T0059867

Erasing Palestine
Free Speech and Palestinian Freedom

Rebecca Ruth Gould

VERSO

London • New York

First published by Verso 2023
© Rebecca Ruth Gould 2023

3 5 7 9 10 8 6 4 2

Verso
UK: 6 Meard Street, London W1F 0EG
US: 388 Atlantic Avenue, Brooklyn, NY 11217
versobooks.com

Verso is the imprint of New Left Books

ISBN-13: 978-1-83976-902-3
ISBN-13: 978-1-83976-903-0 (UK EBK)
ISBN-13: 978-1-83976-904-7 (US EBK)

British Library Cataloguing in Publication Data
A catalogue record for this book is available from the British Library

Library of Congress Cataloging-in-Publication Data

Names: Gould, Rebecca Ruth, author.
Title: Erasing Palestine : free speech and Palestinian freedom / Rebecca
    Ruth Gould.
Other titles: Free speech and Palestinian freedom
Description: London ; New York : Verso, 2023. | Includes bibliographical
    references and index.
Identifiers: LCCN 2023007043 (print) | LCCN 2023007044 (ebook) | ISBN
    9781839769023 (trade paperback) | ISBN 9781839769047 (ebook)
Subjects: LCSH: Antisemitism—Government policy—Great Britain. |
    Antisemitism—History. | Jews—Identity. | Zionism. | Arab-Israeli
    conflict. | Freedom of speech. | Palestine—Politics and
    government—1948- | Great Britain—Foreign relations—Israel. |
    Israel—Foreign relation—Great Britain.
Classification: LCC DS146.G7 G68 2023 (print)
| LCC DS146.G7 (ebook) |
    DDC 305.892/40410904—dc23/eng/20230321
LC record available at https://lccn.loc.gov/2023007043
LC ebook record available at https://lccn.loc.gov/2023007044

Typeset in Sabon by Biblichor Ltd, Scotland
Printed and bound by CPI Group (UK) Ltd, Croydon CR0 4YY

For Christopher Joseph Gould (1949–2022),
lover of free inquiry

'I am . . . a Jew by force of my unconditional solidarity with the persecuted and exterminated.'

Isaac Deutscher, 'Who Is a Jew?' (1966)

Contents

Prologue:
On Being Accused of Antisemitism

February 2017 marked a turning point in the history of Palestinian activism within the UK. In this tumultuous month, Palestinians and pro-Palestine activists were overwhelmed by an unprecedented flurry of event cancellations and attacks on their right to protest against the occupation. February 2017 also marked a turning point in my own involvement with Palestine and free speech. I had arrived in the UK in the summer of 2015 to begin teaching at the University of Bristol. My peripatetic academic career had carried me from Damascus to Berlin, and finally to Palestine and Israel. From 2010 to 2011, I commuted between Palestine and Israel several times a week. I lived in Bethlehem in the West Bank, across from the apartheid wall, along which I walked on my way to the Van Leer Institute where I was a post-doctoral fellow.[1]

The Van Leer Institute is centrally located in the historic Talbia district of West Jerusalem. In another era, thirteen years before the founding of the state of Israel in 1948, Palestinian-American critic Edward Said was born in this neighbourhood. His cousin abandoned the family home in 1948, just after it fell to the Zionist paramilitary Haganah, cutting Said's ties to his homeland for ever.[2] Now, many decades later, the Van Leer Institute has played a pivotal role in debates around definitions of antisemitism. In 2020, it served as the virtual and physical venue for the drafting of the Jerusalem Declaration on Antisemitism (JDA), and hosted many events to support its dissemination.[3]

Although the Van Leer Institute was located just a few kilometres from where I lived, the commute from Bethlehem took several hours. Every morning when I had to travel into Jerusalem, I waited in line with restless and sleep-deprived Palestinian workers at the infamous Checkpoint 300. While standing in line, I would often observe the preferential treatment that I, as a foreigner, experienced from the Israel Defense Forces (IDF) soldiers guarding the checkpoint. The contrast between their treatment of me and natives of Palestine was impossible to ignore. Israeli soldiers allowed me and other foreign passport holders to pass quickly through the metal detectors behind which Palestinian workers often had to stand for hours on end, causing them to be late for work and to lose out on vital income.

Double standards were everywhere on display. The metal barricades behind which we waited had separate rows for foreigners and Palestinians. Different policies applied to each row. During certain hours only foreigners could stand in line. It should not be hard to guess which rows required the longest wait.

Rarely had I seen discrimination so blatantly on display. I evoked these scenes in a few stanzas I wrote at the time:

> Workers greet the dawn
> behind the bars of checkpoint 300,
> waiting to build settlers' homes
> with stolen limestone.[4]

I called this poem 'Stolen Limestone', referring to the alabaster facades of the many buildings that gleamed across the hills of Bethlehem and the neighbouring town of Beit Jala on my way to Jerusalem. These buildings had been constructed by badly remunerated Palestinian labourers, who had to stand in line for hours at checkpoints just to reach the buses that would take them to work.[5] 'Stolen Limestone' dwells on my complicity within the apartheid system that was developing at the time of my residence in Bethlehem, and which has become even more entrenched in the years since my departure.

My salary was funded by a fellowship established by an Israeli philanthropist. In accepting the fellowship, I was in violation of the boycott of Israeli academic institutions in which many of my friends and colleagues were involved. Before accepting it, I debated the ethics of the decision with friends. I wanted to see Palestine – and to live there – first-hand. A five-year fellowship in Jerusalem would make it possible for me to live in Palestine, specifically in nearby Bethlehem in the West Bank, just a few kilometres away. A close friend of mine had recently returned from Bethlehem, and she arranged for an apartment where I could stay. It was potentially a life-changing opportunity to live in Palestine for the long term. I was sympathetic to the boycott, but also felt that I could best contribute to these issues by witnessing the occupation first-hand, and by living it – even if only temporarily.

When it awarded me the fellowship, the Van Leer Institute had no idea that I was planning to live outside Israel and commute into Jerusalem. By the time I arrived in Jerusalem and told them that I would be living in Palestine, it was too late for them to refuse my request. Unlike Israelis, I was legally permitted to reside in the Occupied Territories. Unlike Palestinians, I could enter Jerusalem without seeking special permission. These frequent commutes through congested checkpoints and the exposure to two radically different geographies that abutted each other led me to view the occupation in an entirely different way. This first-hand experience of the occupation intensified and justified my support for the boycott. Until I arrived in Palestine, my support had been based on second-hand information.

It was while living in Bethlehem in the summer of 2011 that I ended up writing a polemical article that condensed all of my frustration with everything I had witnessed in Israel, commuting between Bethlehem and Jerusalem, speaking with Israelis who had never visited the Occupied Territories – which Israeli law prevented them from doing – both observing and inhabiting the bubble in which Israelis live while their Palestinian neighbours experience infinitely greater levels of economic deprivation, unemployment, and violence due to Israeli policies and prejudices.

I lived just blocks from the wall that was being constructed by Israel on a security pretext, even though it ran directly through Palestinian territory. Homes had been cut in two by this stone edifice. Commemorative plaques were erected over the rubble. A few years after I left Bethlehem, these bisecting walls would be memorialized in the Walled Off Hotel, an edifice initially set up by England-based street artist Banksy as a temporary exhibition, eventually becoming a permanent fixture of the occupation. I witnessed heavily armed IDF patrols in the streets, filling Palestinians with fear. I could no longer justify living in – and receiving a livelihood from – this corrupt and discriminatory system. Although I had witnessed the carnage of war first-hand – I had visited Grozny soon after the city was flattened by Russian airstrikes in 2004 – the daily insults and humiliations of Palestinians that I witnessed in the Occupied Territories made me sick. I decided to end my fellowship for the sake of my own sanity.

It was during this time that I wrote a provocatively titled short polemic called 'Beyond Antisemitism'. The work would come back to haunt me many years later, when it propelled me into circumstances that led to the writing of this book. I was furious at myself – among others – for not being able to stop the abuses of history that had normalized the silencing of Palestinian voices. I sent it to the radical left-wing magazine *Counterpunch*. I received a response within hours from the journalist and editor Alexander Cockburn, who passed away the following year. Cockburn liked it, and said that he would feature it in the print edition.[6] A few weeks later, I received a cheque in my mailbox at the Van Leer Institute for $100, with a short note appended thanking me for my contribution. We had never discussed payment terms, and I had never shared my address with Cockburn, so the money came as a surprise.

In retrospect, I can see how the title 'Beyond Antisemitism' might have appeared incendiary, especially when taken out of context. It was calculated to provoke. The title was also chosen to critique the political deployment of the discourse around antisemitism to silence discussion of the occupation of Palestine. I wrote about what I had witnessed first-hand during my residency in Palestine and regular commutes into Israel. I would not have used such a title had I been living anywhere in Europe, where the sites of the twentieth century's greatest atrocity forms a perpetual subtext to every discussion of antisemitism today. But I was not writing from Europe, or indeed anywhere in the UK. I had never even set foot in England at that point in my life. I was writing from Palestine after having worked for a year in Israel, and in frustration at my complicity with the unjust system in which I lived and worked. What, one might wonder, does antisemitism have to do with that? Indirectly, if not explicitly, antisemitism was the pretext for the injustices I witnessed every day against Palestinians. Fear of being accused of antisemitism makes it difficult to speak out, and it is why so many of us who witness anti-Palestinian discrimination – Israelis and non-Israelis alike – keep silent. Our silence is complicity. This complicity also silences Palestinians, keeping their experiences hidden from public view.

'Beyond Antisemitism' argued that the long history of antisemitism and of the Holocaust forms the background against which Palestinian lives are being sacrificed. The idea did not occur to me when I was living in Berlin, before accepting the fellowship from Jerusalem. I discovered this dynamic embedded in the everyday life of Israelis while commuting between my office in Israel and my Palestinian home. The amnesia in which Israelis live reminded me greatly of my own education in the United States. The genocide of Indigenous Americans was thoroughly suppressed in our school curriculums, and slavery was a delicate topic that our teachers avoided discussing directly. The traumas of Jewish history, and the understandable fear that this history might someday repeat itself, had similarly led to distortions and suppressions of the past.

Traumatic memories and the fear of their repetition haunted my conversations with Israelis. These fears fill the airwaves of Israeli radio and shape the cultural memory of the Israeli people. The Israeli state does everything it can to keep the focus on the historical trauma of the Jews. Yet, as Isaac Deutscher remarked in 1967, even when Israel's leaders 'over-exploit Auschwitz and Treblinka . . . We should not allow even invocations of Auschwitz to blackmail us into supporting the wrong cause.'[7] 'Beyond Antisemitism' was a polemic against the forced silences imposed by twentieth-century traumas, which deflect attention away from the occupation of Palestinian lands and the dispossession of the Palestinian people. After a year of residing on the border between Israel and the West Bank, I was certain that there was no justification for the discriminatory checkpoints and segregated bus system, or for the arcane system of passes and regulations that greatly restrict Palestinians' access to employment and keep them in poverty.

While the collateral damage that these memories and fears cause for Palestinians was not forbidden from being discussed in Israeli public spaces, it was treated as secondary, as an afterthought to the more important themes of Jewish history. Meanwhile, alibis for and justifications of the occupation became increasingly untenable. As Deutscher insisted, even invocations of Auschwitz do not legitimate oppression. Even the Jews' long history of antisemitism – in which Palestinians were not directly implicated, yet which nonetheless shape the horizons of their political existence – is no excuse. That is why, I argued in 2011, we needed to move 'beyond antisemitism'.

Among the most controversial parts of the article was the ending, which argued that, 'as the situation stands today, the Holocaust persists and its primary victims are the Palestinian people'.[8] This is admittedly a rather grandiose claim that only works at the polemic level. I think it could be defended in certain ways, but I am less invested in rhetorical triumphs now than I was when writing the piece. It is hardly controversial to insist that historical catastrophes have long-term consequences, stretching across many generations. It is less useful to attempt to claim who is a greater or lesser victim of a specific atrocity generations after the event. The critique of these words that a senior Jewish studies scholar shared with me continues to resonate for me. 'There is no silver lining to the Holocaust,' he said, 'no way of putting a positive spin on it.' I'm not quite sure how he construed my words as looking for silver linings, but I agree with his critique. Foregrounding Palestinian suffering does not work when it seems to make light of Jewish wounds.[9] This was never my intention, and I don't think the text supports that reading, but I respect the right of readers to draw their own conclusions. So I grant that I would have written it differently now, but I stand by the appropriateness of those words for that time and place: occupied Palestine amid an increasingly brutal conflict and an aggressive state-backed mandate to silence dissent. I stand by the outrage that led me to engage in such polemics, and by the right of everyone to do so, be they Palestinian, Israeli, or American.

Another point that concerned some readers was my use of the word 'privilege' to describe the status of the Holocaust narrative within Israel. This verb is used heavily in academic discourse to describe how certain ideas are validated over others. One reader suggested that, given the antisemitic stereotype of Jews as privileged, the use of 'privilege' as a verb with reference to the Holocaust was potentially antisemitic. Read in context, this seems to me far-fetched, given that I was using the verb in its traditional academic sense of setting one viewpoint over another. It was not an ideal choice on aesthetic grounds, but this dry and abstract verb has no specific relationship to Jews.

Soon after completing the article, I resigned from my fellowship and left Israel, never to return. Having vented my rage, I did not give that brief article further thought. It was a polemic, not a work of scholarship. A work of its time, and of my indignation, first and foremost at myself. Writing it was an act of self-denunciation, an attempt to purify myself of my complicity in the occupation, and to purge my guilt at crossing checkpoints using the special lines designated for foreigners, at witnessing racism and discrimination against the Palestinian population while biting my tongue.

Having purged my anger, I moved on to other things. I took up a position with a new liberal arts college called Yale-NUS. Initially it was based on Yale University's campus in New Haven, Connecticut, and then at the National University of Singapore. I took up another fellowship at Central European University, then located in Budapest. Finally, four years after composing that brief polemic, I moved to the UK to take up a position at the University of Bristol in south-west England, where I taught a standard fare of courses in modern languages: Translation Theory, Fourth Year Dissertation Seminar, Postcolonial Theory.

Two years into my position at Bristol, I received a call in my office from the head of school. This was a rare occasion: indeed, she had never called me directly before. She asked me to meet her in her office as soon as I possibly could. She informed me that a student had discovered my 2011 article online, on a database called Social Science Research Network, where I uploaded my work. Among my hundreds of scholarly articles, this short polemic touched a nerve for the student, who identified as a Zionist. She told me that the university had been informed that the student was planning to publish an anonymous letter in the student newspaper, *Epigram*, denouncing my article – and me – as antisemitic. The university administration had been informed of this by the newspaper editor. The university's first reaction was to hope that the story would be quickly buried under other news, and would not be picked up by the national media. Back in 2017, accusations of antisemitism linked to Israel-critical speech were still relatively unusual in the UK. They have since become routine. We, however, were operating in uncharted territory.

Hopes that the controversy would soon pass were misplaced. A few weeks later, a reporter at the *Daily Telegraph* who had made her reputation on clickbait stories accusing various academics of antisemitism, featured the student's 'discovery' of my article in a piece that bore the headline: 'Bristol University Investigates Claims of Anti-Semitism after Lecturer Claims that Jews Should Stop "Privileging" the Holocaust'.[10] One thing I learned from this experience is that, when it comes to reporting, headlines sometimes matter more than substance.

I was sitting in my university office when the phone rang. The reporter, Camilla Turner, asked if I had any comment about 'Beyond Antisemitism', which had been the subject of an anonymous letter in the student newspaper. I requested that she give me a day to respond. She refused, saying that the article was to be posted that evening. So I conferred with the same friend who had found me a place to live in Bethlehem. Together, we combed through the writings of Edward Said, who had long been a guiding light for me, in search of words that could represent what I learned and saw while living in Palestine. My first port of call was Said's classic essay 'Zionism from the Standpoint of Its Victims' (1979). Although the quote I provided to Turner was butchered, at least the core part of Said's message made it into print. 'Denying claims of anti-Semitism Dr Gould quoted Edward W. Said', Turner wrote, and then went on to quote me quoting Said: 'To oppose Zionism in Palestine has never meant, and does not now mean, being anti-Semitic.'

A tempest followed. In the *Telegraph* article about me, Conservative MP and the newly appointed special envoy for post-Holocaust issues Eric Pickles accused me of Holocaust denial. He went so far as to claim that the author of 'Beyond Antisemitism' should 'consider her position' at the university, which was a polite British way of saying I should either resign or be fired. Even more astonishingly, he described my article as 'one of the worst cases of Holocaust denial' that he had seen in recent years. While the newly created Campaign Against Antisemitism had been the first organization to call for my dismissal, and indeed had initiated its campaign against me prior to the *Telegraph* and probably collaborated with Turner on the article, the more established Board of Deputies of British Jews joined the chorus. The Board of Deputies wrote to the vice chancellor about me, claiming in a letter concealed from me by the university for many years, that my views were 'incompatible with the role of a teacher at a reputable British university', and insisting that I 'should no longer remain in post'.[11]

Ironically, one hundred years earlier, in a radically different era, this same Board of Deputies that now called for my dismissal had been among the signatories to express concerns about the British government's increasing support for Zionism. In a controversial letter to *The Times* dated 24 May 1917, the Board of Deputies, together with the Anglo-Jewish Association, objected to the 'Zionist theory, which regards all the Jewish communities of the world as constituting one homeless nationality, incapable of complete social and political identification with the nations among whom they dwelt'.[12] The signatories worried about the implications of conceiving of all Jews as members of a single 'homeless nationality', since this in itself might create 'a political center and an always available homeland in Palestine', protesting 'strongly and earnestly' against this theory. That letter from 1917 was to mark the end of the Board of Deputies' acceptance of anti-Zionism as a legitimate position for Jews. By 2017, the Board of Deputies had completely shed its past scepticism towards the Zionist project, and wholeheartedly embraced a nationalist conception of the Jewish people, even lobbying for the dismissal of those who did not agree with them.

It was only a few weeks later that the identity of the student who had accused me of antisemitism was revealed, in an interview he gave to the *Huffington Post*. The way in which he turned himself into the hero of the fiasco suggested something about his motivations from the beginning. In the interview, he said he did not want to see me fired. He speculated that I had only represented Israel in such a negative way because I had never before encountered a Zionist Jew like him. He expressed satisfaction at having played a role in my enlightenment. I had worked in Israel for a year, and the article in question was written while I was living in Palestine, yet the student seemed oblivious or indifferent to these details. In this respect, his reaction correlated with that of nearly every other UK observer.

While the student was busy claiming the limelight for what he perceived as his heroic defence of academic freedom, no one asked for my perspective on these events. Media commentators showed little interest in learning about the Palestinians who were most severely silenced by the crackdown on Israel-critical dissent. Time and again, reporters presented me with binary questions. Did I or did I not retract my article? Did I accept the right of the state of Israel to exist? Did I acknowledge the legitimacy of Zionism? As to the first, there was nothing for me to retract. What I witnessed while living in Palestine and commuting into Israel was no illusion, and my words were not fiction. I had to stand by them.

Anti-Zionism is the opposition to a certain kind of nationalism that has resulted in the dispossession of Palestinians. Antisemitism is animosity towards Jews as Jews. There is no causal link between the two positions, and neither implies the other. Yet, precisely because there is no causal link, it is also true that neither excludes the other. They can coexist, just like sets any of unrelated ideas and prejudices. Exasperated by the sloganeering in both directions, I chose silence.

This book chronicles the destructive forces that the pressure to adopt the so-called IHRA definition of antisemitism has unleashed within British society. Since so many aspects of the definition have been misrepresented and misreported, it is necessary to dwell on the circumstances of its genesis and adoption, before resuming the story of my first encounter with it in 2017.

The Politics of a Name:
The IHRA Definition of Antisemitism

The politics of naming partly explain the widespread acceptance of the twenty-first-century definition of antisemitism that has reframed – and constrained – the debate around Israel in recent years. A few of the key acronyms that recur throughout this story should be introduced at this juncture; first, the European Monitoring Centre on racism and xenophobia (EUMC), an early incarnation of the European Union's Agency for Fundamental Rights; second, the International Holocaust Remembrance Alliance (IHRA), from which the IHRA definition takes its name. Anyone following the fortunes of the Labour Party since 2015 will have heard many times of the IHRA definition, although they may not know why it is referred to in that way.[13] A number of other acronyms also feature less prominently in this story: the Conjoint Foreign Committee (CFC), the American Jewish Committee (AJC), the UK-based Community Security Trust (CST), and the Simon Wiesenthal Center (SWC).

Although the proliferation of acronyms suggests a story of bewildering complexity, the main thread of this narrative is simple: the definition of antisemitism that was adopted by the EUMC in 2005 is identical to the version that was adopted by the IHRA in 2016, with a few caveats. The most significant difference between these two – the perceived relation between the definition and the supporting examples – relates less to the definition's content than to its formal applications. The difference pertains to the EUMC and IHRA definitions' perceived purpose, legitimacy, and hence power. More than the EUMC definition, the IHRA definition targets what is referred to as 'the new antisemitism', by which is meant antisemitic criticism focused on Israel dating roughly to the start of the second Palestinian intifada in 2000. The accuracy of this label has been widely disputed by scholars such as Brian Klug, who pithily writes that it is 'not necessary to consult a logic manual to see that the inference' that hostility to Zionism must be antisemitic 'involves a fallacy'.[14] Notwithstanding the logical flaws, the assumption that hostility to Zionism is antisemitic is the distinguishing feature of this definition, which has been associated with many different institutions, including the EUMC, the IHRA, and the US State Department.[15] Yet all of these definitions that target the new antisemitism are essentially different names for the same censorious content. The only thing that separates them from each other is their names.

Why has the same definition appeared under so many different names? The shifting nomenclature is a key to its success. In the early years of the twenty-first century, the American Jewish Committee convened a group of lawyers and academics to formulate a more comprehensive, robust, and institutionally relevant definition of antisemitism than any that had existed to that date. The absence of a widely recognized definition of antisemitism in public policy and policing was, in the view of these drafters, one reason why antisemitic crimes were not being classified as hate crimes. The group that drafted the new definition included several AJC employees: Ken Stern, program specialist on antisemitism and extremism; Rabbi Andrew Baker, director of international Jewish affairs; Deidre Berger, senior European affairs advisor; and Felice Gaer, director of the AJC's Jacob Blaustein Institute for the Advancement of Human Rights. Other members of the group included Dina Porat, professor of modern Jewish history at Tel Aviv University and chief historian at Yad Vashem (the Jewish Holocaust Museum); Michael Whine, the director of government and international affairs at the Community Security Trust (CST); Michael Berenbaum of the US Holocaust Memorial Museum; Yehuda Bauer of Hebrew University; and Ronnie Stauber of Tel Aviv University.[16] The group was a mix of academic and policy advocates.

The definition drafted by this committee during 2004 was the first to draw a formal link between criticism of Israel and antisemitism. This linkage was partly a reaction against a current in international geopolitics that denominated Zionism as a form of racism, and Israel as an apartheid state. This perspective on Zionism is often associated with the United Nations' World Conference Against Racism, which took place in Durban, South Africa, in 2001. At the Durban conference, a number of formerly colonized countries agreed to define Zionism as a form of racism. They reiterated their position at a follow-up conference, also in Durban, in 2009. It was in this climate that the new definition of antisemitism gained traction.

The first paragraph of the new antisemitism definition opened with a straightforward assertion: 'Antisemitism is hatred towards Jews because they are Jews and is directed towards the Jewish religion and Jews individually or collectively.' So far, there is nothing hugely objectionable, even though the text fails as a definition of anything. Yet it was the next qualification that was to prove most controversial: 'Most recently, antisemitism has been manifested in the demonization of the state of Israel.'[17] This last sentence was an innovation. The Israeli government recognized this, noting in a report from 2017: 'the main innovation in the working definition is that it also includes expressions of Antisemitism directed against the State of Israel'.[18] The added clause about Israel, which is by far the most controversial aspect of the definition, fit with the wider agenda of the advocacy groups that had been involved in crafting the new definition since its inception.

The explicit invocation of anti-Israel discourse as a form of antisemitism was removed from the draft of the definition that came to be associated with – though never adopted by – the EUMC. That version, which was briefly posted on the EUMC website and later removed, read: 'Anti-Semitism is a certain perception of Jews, which may be expressed as hatred towards Jews. Rhetorical and physical manifestations of anti-Semitism are directed toward Jewish or non-Jewish individuals and/or their property, toward Jewish community institutions and religious facilities.' This altered text is considerably vaguer as a definition.

It shifts from 'anti-Semitism is hatred' to 'anti-Semitism is a *certain perception* . . . which *may* be expressed as hatred'.[19] Both 'certain perception' and 'may' make this formulation less usable in the task of identifying what antisemitism is, since a definition should be concerned with what something *is*, rather than with what it 'may' be. But the main difference between the first and second formulations is with regard to Israel, which is mentioned in the version proposed by the AJC but is missing from the version that was associated with the EUMC.

The story of the association between Israel and this new definition of antisemitism does not end here. It was through the EUMC definition that the association between the 'new antisemitism' and the critique of Israel would come to shape the policies and practices of governments and public institutions, ultimately leading them to censor speech critical of Israel. The association with Israel was retained, even after it was excised from the definition itself. Its placement simply changed. Instead of being invoked in the definition proper, Israel was invoked in the first of the supporting examples, which read: 'such manifestations could also target the state of Israel, conceived as a Jewish collectivity'.

In an open letter addressed to the secretary general of the IHRA and the European Commission coordinator on combating antisemitism and fostering Jewish life, members of the collective who had drafted the original definition noted that it 'was not meant to be a tool for academic researchers, but for those . . . who would put it to use'.[20] By this point, the group had parted ways with Ken Stern, the author of the core definition, who would later become one of the most prominent critics of its misapplications.[21] A 2011 report commemorating the six-year anniversary of the drafting of the definition made the same point: the working definition, state Dina Porat and Esther Webman, 'is not a theoretical academic' definition; rather, it 'aims at being a practical guide for identifying antisemitism'.[22] The implied distinction between 'academic' and 'practical' is not clear, to me at least, but if it is intended as a blunt political instrument rather than an accurate description of reality, the new definition of antisemitism has served its purpose well. Ignoring the historically contingent nature of antisemitism, the definition avoids inquiring into 'the reasons and developments from which antisemitism originates' in order to focus instead on how to identify and prevent it.

Once the definition was drafted, Baker approached the EUMC director, Beate Winkler, in the hope of securing institutional backing for it. According to some reports, the EUMC agreed to have the definition associated with its name in order to avoid negative publicity from a leaked antisemitism report that had placed unwelcome emphasis on anti-Jewish hate crimes perpetrated by Muslims.[23] For a period of nine years, the definition was loosely affiliated with this EU agency and appeared on its website. When EUMC officials were queried, however, they insisted that the definition had not been officially 'adopted'. Indeed, the very idea of institutional adoption belongs to a later phase in the definition's trajectory, after the EUMC definition was renamed the IHRA definition.

So long as the definition was associated with the EUMC, the concept of 'adoption', which would require the definition to be applied to specific statements or utterances in order to determine whether they fell outside the pale of legitimate expression, had yet to be codified. When the EUMC removed the definition from its website, the break was clear.[24] The definition needed a new institutional home, and a new name. The International Holocaust Remembrance Alliance, an organization founded in 1998 by former Swedish prime minister Göran Persson with the aim of promoting the memory of the Holocaust and finding ways to prevent its reoccurrence, was to fill that gap.

Conveniently, Mark Weitzman, director of government affairs at an Israel-advocacy organization called the Simon Wiesenthal Center, was also chair of the IHRA's Committee on Antisemitism and Holocaust Denial in 2014. He used his position to advocate for the adoption of what had until then been called the EUMC definition. Although the exact meaning of 'adoption' was still ambiguous, it was pursued by the entire IHRA, including (eventually) most of its thirty-one member countries, ranging across Europe and the Americas. Rather disingenuously, given the history of the definition that preceded him and in which he was not directly involved, the SWC credits Weitzman as 'the "architect" of the IHRA definition and one of the principal figures in shaping and introducing this definition of antisemitism'.[25]

The text of the EUMC definition was proposed to the IHRA in 2015 and adopted soon after, in May 2016. It was under this new guise – but with hardly any alteration – that the IHRA definition assumed the form in which we know it today. 'IHRA', a name that ought to be associated with Holocaust memory, is an odd fit for a definition that focuses in practice on criminalizing anti-Israel speech. The IHRA was not founded for the purpose of Israel advocacy. But ever since Weitzman acquired a leadership position within this organization, it appears to have been hijacked by an Israel-advocacy agenda. The IHRA has played a significant role in obscuring from public view key details about the relationship between the definition and the examples.[26]

The UK was the first country in the world to adopt the newly branded IHRA definition. The adoption was announced on 12 December 2016 by Conservative party leader and prime minister Theresa May. The mainstream media barely took notice. Professor David Feldman, director of Birkbeck University's Pears Institute for the Study of Antisemitism, was one of the few who made a public statement on the occasion of the adoption.[27] His words turned out to be prophetic. 'The greatest flaw of the IHRA definition', Feldman wrote just weeks after the adoption, 'is its failure to make any ethical and political connections between the struggle against antisemitism and other sorts of prejudice. On behalf of Jews it dares to spurn solidarity with other groups who are the targets of bigotry and hatred.'[28] Feldman's was the best – and certainly the most prescient – analysis of the definition to date, yet it fell on deaf ears. Four years later, Feldman would become one of the drafters and most articulate supporters of the

Jerusalem Declaration on Antisemitism, which was proposed as a corrective to the IHRA definition on 25 March 2021.

Within months of the UK government's adoption of the IHRA definition, the SWC, along with other UK-based organizations such as the Campaign Against Antisemitism, began campaigning against anti-Israel protests, such as Israel Apartheid Week, claiming that the adoption of the IHRA definition mandated their cancellation. Pro-Palestine advocates were caught by surprise. Many sudden cancellations of Israel-critical events occurred across UK campuses during the spring of 2017. When an event on Palestine was cancelled at the University of Central Lancashire in February 2017, the Simon Wiesenthal Center immediately claimed credit, arguing that all other universities should likewise use the definition to get anti-Israel events cancelled. In the aftermath of this crackdown, politicians such as Labour MP John Mann and other defenders of the IHRA definition claimed that these crackdowns on pro-Palestinian activism were examples of the misuse of the IHRA. When properly implemented, they claimed, the IHRA definition posed no threat to freedom of expression. These proponents were on shaky ground, given that the Simon Wiesenthal Center, the very organization that had spearheaded the definition's adoption, promoted its use precisely to cancel anti-Israel protests.

Let us now turn to the IHRA definition's content. The elaborate four-letter acronym is already obscure to many outsiders to the debate and masks what is actually at stake in this term. The fact that 'IHRA' stands for International Holocaust Remembrance Alliance, and that this organization agreed to promote the definition in 2015, tells us almost nothing about how it emerged, what it is, or why it matters. The association of this definition with the International Holocaust Remembrance Alliance is a late development in its history, which took place just before I was briefly at the epicentre of the UK debate around criticism of Israel and Palestine advocacy.[29] While the association of the definition with the IHRA was politically instrumental in facilitating its widespread adoption by a number of countries and government agencies, intellectually it is of negligible significance, because the definition had existed decades earlier under various names.

Simply put, the IHRA definition is a two-part construction consisting of a simple if not particularly illuminating rendition of what antisemitism is ('a certain perception of Jews, which may be expressed as hatred toward Jews') and a much more controversial set of eleven examples of how antisemitism manifests itself in society and public discourse. Of these eleven examples, seven refer to Israel, and feature contentious elements, such as 'Denying the Jewish people their right to self-determination, e.g., by claiming that the existence of a State of Israel is a racist endeavor.' It is the second part of this two-part construction, which is not strictly part of the definition but is often incorrectly referred to as such, that has proved so problematic, and has been invoked during the past decade to justify firing critics of Israel, censoring their work, and denying them the right to express their views.

In this book, I refer to the IHRA definition as 'nominalist' (alternatively 'idealist'), by which I mean that it reduces antisemitism to a phenomenon that exists in the realm of mental abstraction rather than in material conditions. The opening phrase – 'a certain perception of Jews' – demonstrates this point by suggesting that antisemitism begins in the mind and is only later expressed in material reality. By calling the IHRA definition nominalist, I highlight the wider problem with its understanding of antisemitism – a problem that is also found in other idealist approaches to racism. The label 'nominalist' moves us beyond the critique of specific examples, which is important but inadequate for dislodging its toxic influence, as we work to develop a more effective framework for combating antisemitism and other forms of racism. At least as problematic as the IHRA definition's examples is the tendency of its supporters to understand antisemitism as a discourse that originates in speech rather than in material conditions. In this respect the IHRA definition is hardly alone; idealism besets the definitional mentality which has taken root more generally in UK government circles, amid increasing calls for group-specific definitions of racism. In place of this definitional nominalism, I advocate a materialist critique of anti-semitism – and of other racisms – that is attentive to class, histories of discrimination, and the political economy. This materialist critique of antisemitism – explored particularly in Chapter 3 – is critical of dominant economic interests and respectful of freedom of speech.

From Chaos to Bureaucracy

On 19 April 2017, two months after I was accused of anti-semitism in the student newspaper, a university panel comprising three professors convened to assess the claim that my article was antisemitic. Despite my lawyer's protests, the committee's com-position was kept secret from me. I was told only that these professors were guided by the university lawyer. I was also informed, in a rather absurd formulation, that at least one pro-fessor would represent 'the Jewish perspective' while another would represent 'the human rights perspective'. The implied opposition between these two perspectives was jarring, since I was not accustomed to thinking of them as opposed to each other; but I kept that objection to myself. When I asked the uni-versity's legal counsel, 'What about the Palestinian perspective?', she responded that it would be folded into the human-rights perspective. As so often happens in university contexts where Palestinians are rarely seen on campus, Palestinian voices and perspectives were neatly elided by rhetorical erasure – a process we will see repeated time and again in the context of the struggle for Palestinian freedom.

The remit of the panel was to consider 'both the text of the article and . . . the wider social and political contexts relevant to that evaluation'.[30] For the panel, this meant the UK in 2017 – not the Palestinian and Israeli context in 2011, in which it had been written. The panel produced a four-page assessment of my article, which was longer than the piece itself. The report was issued less than six months after the UK government's adoption of the IHRA definition – to which, in deference to the government mandate, the panellists announced their intention to give 'detailed and close attention'. As this commitment indicates, Bristol University deferred to the definition *before* it had been widely adopted on UK campuses. To the best of my knowledge, the panel report on my article was the first formal invocation of the IHRA definition on any UK university campus, and possibly on any campus anywhere in the world. In 2020, UK parliamentarian John Mann would claim that the IHRA definition 'doesn't restrict free speech'.[31] His argument had already been disproved three years earlier by this 2017 report.

The shadow that the IHRA definition cast over the panel report set a precedent for many further incidents of censorship, event cancellations, and violations of academic freedom and freedom of speech that followed. As a participant in these proceedings – indeed, as their object – what struck me most was that even those who invoked the definition in order to protect themselves and their position could perceive its flaws. When they invoked the definition, they were not acting out of conviction or belief. They were thinking strategically about what the government wanted, not about what the fight against antisemitism required. They knew better than to trust the definition as a barometer for gauging actual antisemitism; and yet they applied it nonetheless, because it felt politically necessary. I say this not in order to indict specific individuals, but because I believe that the bureaucratic application of this definition in a way that severs it from any meaningful ethical context is likely to be repeated in any heavily regulated institutional environment. It is in the nature of speech codes that they tend to be bureaucratized to the point where the impulse behind their genesis – the initial intention of opposing racism – is lost, and their function becomes merely to demonstrate compliance with a government mandate. Among other official documents, the appendix to the panel report referenced a letter to Universities UK from Jo Johnson, the minister of state for universities, science, research and innovation.[32] In that letter, which would turn out to be the first among many ministerial interventions on the subject of the IHRA definition, Johnson informed the chief executive of Universities UK, Nicola Dandridge, that the UK government had recently adopted the IHRA definition of antisemitism.

On the face of it, there is nothing particularly alarming about Johnson's statement. It reads as a neutral letter, citing only the IHRA definition and omitting the examples. The tone of neutrality holds until the fifth paragraph, when Johnson singles out 'events that might take place under the banner of "Israel Apartheid"' as calling for a special kind of scrutiny. He does not directly insist that universities adopt the definition, but rather notes that the definition is 'intended to help front-line services better understand and recognise instances of anti-Semitism'. It is easy to see in retrospect why Johnson's letter did not attract the scrutiny it merited when it was first circulated: its tone is muted and bureaucratic, almost as if the goal was to suppress dissent through boredom rather than public denunciation. The full implications of Johnson's ministerial letter only became clear three years and many ministers later, when Gavin Williamson, secretary of state for education under Boris Johnson, wrote to the vice chancellor of every UK university threatening to withdraw their funding if they refused to adopt the IHRA definition.[33] Four months later, Williamson followed up on this threat by requesting that the Office of Students – a new public body that had recently been created to regulate the higher education sector – 'identify providers which are reluctant to adopt the definition'. Institutions that had not yet adopted the definition should be closely monitored and potentially fined.[34] The Office of Students then published a list of institutions that had adopted the definition on its website, presumably with the aim of pressuring any institutions which had not yet done so.[35] When he took these drastic steps, Williamson was building on a tradition of silencing pro-Palestinian activism that had been pioneered by a long series of Conservative ministers, from Johnson to Chris Skidmore, Michelle Donelan, and Nadhim Zahawi.

Although Williamson placed himself on the moral high ground as a proponent of the IHRA definition and sought to shame universities into adopting it, his letter did not register the fact that adopting a definition by itself would do nothing to prevent antisemitism. Rather, the application of pressure through threats of withdrawing funding was the government's way of exerting control over what can and cannot be said on UK university campuses. Even the corporate law firm Shakespeare Martineau, known for representing institutions of higher education in their legal disputes with employees, called Williamson's threat to withdraw funding from universities that failed to adopt the definition 'straight out of Trump's playbook'.[36]

Five years of witnessing the UK government's weaponization of free-speech rhetoric designed to create the illusion that it was combating antisemitism have taught me not to take at face value any official statement about combating antisemitism or any kind of racism. It is hardly unsurprising that governments fail to take free speech seriously, given that the most important function of free speech is to enable dissent from government mandates. The deception, manipulation, and antidemocratic coercion with which the IHRA definition of antisemitism has come to be associated in the UK has deprived the definition of any credibility it might otherwise have retained. It has called into question the entire project of defining racism for governmental and, in university contexts, disciplinary ends.

Finally, the widespread adoption of the IHRA definition and the internalization of its norms has set in motion a simplistic definitional logic for dealing with social problems that has impoverished discussions of racism and prejudice more generally, across the UK and beyond. It has encouraged a focus on words over substance, on censorship over freedom of speech and intellectual honesty. Every time a pro-Palestine event is cancelled or an activist is censored under the guise of compliance with the IHRA definition, and hence with governmental aims, we are taught not to trust what the state says about itself and its commitment to our freedoms. Under the IHRA definition, fighting antisemitism has become an empty performance, undertaken for political gain.

In this book, I tell the story of how this has happened, with a focus on internal politics within the UK over the course of the past several years. In order to tell that story, I also have to engage with a much longer one about the history of antisemitism since the beginning of the twentieth century. I also have to tell a story about Palestine, even though the story reads like a chronicle of erasure more than a narrative history. Finally, I have to tell a story about free speech, and why it matters to Palestinian freedom. In other words, I have to do more than any single book can do. Rather than trying to be comprehensive, I have chosen to tell my story through snapshots and scenes, as fragments of suppressed histories that we collectively have to connect. Stylistically and aesthetically, I have had to break with the scholarly traditions in which I have been trained. I have not cited every single source that might be relevant to these issues, and have opted for narrative rather than argument when it helped to get my point across. I have tried to write in such a way as to give you, dear reader, a visceral sense of what is at stake in these sometimes abstract and remote debates, and why they actually matter, now and in the future.

The very book you hold in your hands attests to the ongoing costs that are extracted from such accusations, long after the person accused has been formally vindicated. This book could not be published without legal review, and, no matter how positive the outcome, such procedures are costly, both to the author and publisher. There are many even more troubling examples, too, including the case of Palestinian scholar Shahd Abusalama, who left Sheffield Hallam University *after* she was cleared by the university, because she was exposed to repeated investigations on the same charges while the university fostered an unwelcome environment.[37] In the censorious environment created by the IHRA definition, even those who do not lose their jobs and who are widely recognized to have been wrongly accused are by no means protected.

Like everyone, I am limited in my ability to represent what is beyond my immediate experience, including the suffering of Palestinians within Palestine and of other peoples who find themselves on the wrong side of history. I write from the perspective of multiple kinds of privilege: of a white, middle-class migrant from the US to the UK who has had the luxury of more or less being able to dedicate herself to ideas that have struck her as most central to our collective freedom. My privileges of race, class, and nationality, as well as simple luck, have no doubt blinded me in certain ways and predetermined my preoccupations. It is in the places where my various privileges – as an American resident in the UK, as a middle-class white person, as a university professor – broke down that my interest has been most sustained. I wrote this book because, for a brief episode in my life, I learned that my privileges did not protect me from being summarily dismissed from my position for no other reason than that I had given voice to controversial views and spoken out against apartheid.

Of course there are people – in Palestine, in Iran, in China, in Russia, indeed in most authoritarian states – who live without these protections not just on rare occasions, but consistently over the course of their entire lives. They cannot assume that human rights will protect them from prison, injustice, or discrimination. There is no higher tribunal to which they can appeal, no international court of human rights that has genuine legal force. Many of them suffer economic deprivation due to the unjust circumstances in which they find themselves. Many others are imprisoned, and some even die, due to their refusal to self-censor, or to compromise on their convictions. I, by contrast, emerged relatively unscathed from what was nonetheless a harrowing and surreal experience that was fraught with fear. But one experience I share in common with these brave individuals who have endured much more than I have is that I understand the value and purpose of free speech. That understanding was stamped on my consciousness when I was threatened with dismissal from my position at the University of Bristol.

My commitment to free speech did not come through ideology. It was not a belief that I was born with. Rather, free speech was something I took for granted, like many Europeans and North Americans. Prior to being accused of antisemitism, I believed that, as a society, we had moved beyond the 1960s, when free speech was a battle cry on the left. In other words, I thought that free speech had already been achieved, and that the struggle for its realization belonged to the past. I believed that we should instead focus on racial, social, and economic equality, and leave free speech issues to conservatives who preferred to debate 'cancel culture'.

I still believe that racial, social, and economic equality should take priority. If the state cannot achieve equality of opportunity for everyone, then it has no right to exist, in my view. But I no longer see free speech as peripheral to the achievement of equality, to the defeat of racism, or to any other aspect of social justice. I now see how free speech, by its very nature, undermines authoritarianism. And I see this not because I read it in a book on the subject, but because I lived and I continue to live in a society that is in the grip of authoritarianism on matters relating to Palestine and Israel. In other spheres, the UK and the US are far ahead of authoritarian regimes in terms of how they treat dissidents, but on this specific issue, there is a great deal more parity. Having seen up close how systematically free speech is suppressed by those in power, I can now see more clearly how essential it is in resistance against tyranny, however privileged or disenfranchised one happens to be.

In the pages that follow, I examine the uses that Jews and Palestinians engaged in the struggle for freedom have made of their right to dissent, in the process developing a 'ruthless criticism of all that exists', to quote Karl Marx.[38] I introduce their views, and sometimes delve deep into the past, in order to illuminate their relevance to our political present. This prologue has narrated the beginning of my engagement with the critique of antisemitism. Chapter 1 documents the erasure of Palestine that has coincided with the widespread adoption of a new understanding of antisemitism during the past two decades. Chapter 2 traces how the critique of antisemitism has developed in relation to the idea of Palestine, and has increasingly been incorporated into a Zionist narrative, since the Balfour Declaration of 1917. Chapter 3 draws on anti-Zionist critiques of antisemitism – in particular, the groundbreaking yet forgotten analysis of Leon Abram – to develop a materialist approach to antisemitism that I believe is better suited to our political present than the definition-based approaches that dominate discourse today. Chapter 4 examines the relationship between free speech and Palestinian freedom, focusing in particular on North American and British universities during the past few decades. In the Epilogue, I conclude by returning to my personal biography, reflecting on how being accused of antisemitism led me to confront my family's suppressed Jewish past.

I hope that these snapshots of my intellectual journey to understand the histories that entangled me in the ongoing erasure of Palestine will lead to different ways of thinking about the rights and privileges we tend to take for granted within liberal democracies. These include our freedoms and civil liberties and the inadvertent contributions that we make to their suppression, both at home and abroad, including within Palestine. This book is partly a story of my conversion to free speech as a discourse central to my own humanity, but also as a value that is inextricably linked to Palestinian freedom. It is a polemic for free speech in places and contexts from which it is gradually disappearing, as well as an attempt to outline how activists on the left can reclaim free speech as our birthright. Finally, it is a call for a materialist approach to antisemitism and other racisms that is less susceptible to being hijacked by government bureaucracies than its idealist counterparts. Although the story takes place within a university, it reaches well beyond the walls of the academy, and the reader will see that I am in general quite sceptical of the potential of any institution – including institutions of higher education – to bring about political liberation.

If you have the misfortune to be targeted for expressing your convictions, I hope this book will remind you that you are not alone in being singled out and persecuted. May the histories chronicled in these pages give you the resources to connect your struggles with those of the activists and writers who preceded us, often under circumstances even more challenging than those we face today. May the conjuncture of past and present create new paths for Palestinian liberation. And may we learn to use the lessons of free speech struggles in times past to advance the liberation of all oppressed peoples.

1

Erasing Palestine

While the redefinition of antisemitism has transformed the conversation around Israel during the twenty-first century, Palestine itself has been gradually erased from the map, its territory continually annexed by Israel. Palestinian artist Sliman Mansour (b. 1947) depicts this process graphically in his artwork from 1996 entitled *Shrinking Object*, which is depicted on the cover of this book. The technique used in this work of art, which is made of mud on wood, was developed during the First Intifada (1987–93), at a time when Palestinian artists were boycotting art supplies from Israel as part of a wider boycott of Israeli goods.

Since their boycott prevented them from using traditional paint, Palestinian artists turned to their natural environment, and started creating art with materials at hand, such as mud, wood, leather, and found objects. The reliance on materials from nature serves this work well, bringing into relief how the shrinking of Palestine appears on Palestinian land, far from maps that are manufactured to conceal the shrinkage and to create the illusion of peace. The earthy materials in this work of art tell a different story, which belies the narrative of international law and diplomacy that continues to invest in an illusory two-state solution.

The map of Palestine is being redrawn, often in ways rendered more lucidly by Palestinian artists than in geopolitical cartography. Yet, even as it is abstracted from its territory, the dismemberment of Palestine is taking place in full view of the world. Palestine is perpetually being reconfigured and reassembled to accommodate external agendas. Whenever Israel attacks Gaza, or there is an act of resistance in the Occupied Territories, Palestine features in the headlines of the world's newspapers and news networks. These inclusions are more often than not pejorative, and used to legitimate Israel's settler-colonial enterprise, often within the framework of the War on Terror.[1] Erasure does not equate with disappearance, however. Palestine remains present, even ubiquitous, while Palestinians undergo deformation, defamation, and systematic manipulation.

Palestine's erasure is taking place in three ways. First, this erasure takes place through acts of renaming, as when the United States relocated its embassy to Jerusalem, thereby recognizing Israel's sovereignty over the city and denying Palestinians' deep links to it. Other acts of renaming include the labelling of Palestinians as Arabs, thereby denying their national heritage and claims on the lands that have been taken from them. Renaming also happens when peacefully protesting Palestinians are redefined as terrorists. Second, erasure takes the form of the fragmentation of space, as exemplified by the wall built by the Israeli state that bisects Palestinian cities and homes, cutting off families and communities from each other.

A third erasure happens in the domain of speech and expression, and it encompasses not just Palestinians but all advocates of the Palestinian cause. It is the dark side of the IHRA definition, which not only censors Israel-critical speech, but also causes Palestinian perspectives to be viewed as presumptively antisemitic. Palestine is erased in the domain of speech when certain forms of Palestinian advocacy are forbidden, banned, or deemed illegitimate. This linguistic reconfiguration is increasingly accomplished through the redefinition of antisemitism, which is conflated with criticism of Israel and advocacy for Palestine. The physical erasure of Palestine coincides with its erasure through language; once Palestinian identity has been successfully suppressed, it becomes that much easier to erase Palestinian claims on Israeli-occupied land.

Since erasure takes place through languages, the work of resistance must also be carried out through language, by resisting censorship and reframing free speech to make it better serve the cause of Palestinian freedom. But analytical reframing is only a small part of the work that needs to be done. In this chapter, I make the connection between the definition of antisemitism and the politics of free speech by means of a brief journey to contemporary Palestine. I look at how the reshaping of the physical geography of Palestine correlates with the worldwide redefinition of antisemitism, and with the rewriting of Jewish history so as to boost Israel's territorial claims.[2] As in my discussions of antisemitism and free speech, I am concerned here with representations – in this case, representations of Palestinians through their own artistic productions, especially in film and literature. While these pages cannot represent the Palestinian experience or its erasure in depth or detail, this discussion may serve, like Mansour's *Shrinking Object*, as a reminder of what is happening on the ground within Palestine. While civil liberties are being violated in the so-called western world as a result of the occupation of Palestine, lives are being lost within Palestine itself.

On 6 December 2017, less than a year after the UK's adoption of the IHRA definition, Donald Trump's announcement that the United States would be moving its embassy to Jerusalem stirred outrage around the world. In practice, Trump's proposal was simply a continuation of a policy to which the US Congress had committed itself in 1995, when it passed the Jerusalem Embassy Act.[3] This act committed the United States to relocating its embassy to Jerusalem at an undefined future date. Ever since the passage of the act, US presidents have promised to implement it. Although it shocked the world, Trump's approach was more a fulfilment of well-established US foreign policy than an departure from it. From this vantage point, the embassy move activates a status quo that has prevailed since the founding of Israel in 1948, and which has become even more normalized since 1967. Some have even argued that the move merely makes more apparent an apartheid system that had been operating de facto for decades.

In understanding the significance of the embassy move, what goes unstated by US policymakers is just as important as what is spoken out loud. 'While the announcement dramatically heralds the US intention to regard Jerusalem as the Israeli capital', notes Mick Dumper, 'it did not specify what geographical areas constituted that capital'.[4] Not unlike the global redefinition of antisemitism encapsulated in the IHRA definition, the movement of the US embassy to Jerusalem was first and foremost a symbolic act. While US states are actively incorporating variations on the IHRA definition into their legal documents and outlawing support for the BDS movement, US foreign policy is solidifying Israel's territorial claims on the international stage. Meanwhile, the borders of the newly reconfigured Jerusalem remain undelineated in spatial terms. In announcing the embassy move, the office of the president claimed that the United States was not taking any 'position on borders or boundaries' with respect to Israel.[5]

Perhaps the plan was first to make the rhetorical transformation into a reality, and then – only then – to allow the facts on the ground to change. Executed in this way, the erasure could be made to appear as a nonviolent act, and the opportunity to protest its outcome in the long term would be greatly reduced. Through such modes of censorship and vaguely symbolic border reconfigurations, and by means of evasions that mirror on the ground the work of the IHRA definition in language, the erasure of Palestine is made to appear like an irrevocable and even natural process, impervious to human intervention.

Erasing Time: Palestinian Checkpoints

On an average day, a Palestinian who works in Jerusalem and resides in the West Bank must wake up at four in the morning in order to arrive at work by nine. The reason is not the distance between workplace and home. With the construction of the separation wall that began in 2002, and is still underway as of 2022, the Israeli state entered into a new stage of encroachment on Palestinian territory.[6] The Palestinian worker has to wait in line for hours at checkpoints staffed by soldiers who are incentivized to make the line move as slowly as possible. Most of these border-crossers have a long day ahead of them in various kinds of construction work. After crossing into Israel, they must spend hours every day passing through checkpoints to get to work, even though they often have only a few kilometres to travel.

The short distance traversed by Palestinian workers who commute from the West Bank into Israel for work encompasses one of the most humiliating and dangerous journeys that can be undertaken by any human being. Recent films by Palestinian filmmakers shed light on the ongoing paradoxes of occupation. In *200 Meters* (2020), Ameen Nayfeh chronicles the short but dangerous journey of the protagonist, Mustafa, as he travels a mere 200 metres in the boot of a car. The film is set in the Palestinian city of Tulkaram, which was one of the first cities to be bisected by the Israeli separation barrier. Mustafa needs to cross the Israel–Palestine border in order to see his son, who has been hospitalized by a car crash. He has to pay a smuggler to get him across the border, and nearly dies of suffocation on the way. He ends up journeying hundreds of kilometres, scaling walls, going undercover, and risking his life simply to get to the other side of the nearby border. Unlike in many comparable films, the protagonist's journey is not far: the challenge he faces is how to cross a border a few miles away.

From September 2011 to June 2012, I lived in Bethlehem, just around the corner from Checkpoint 300, also known as the Gilo Checkpoint after the name of a nearby Jewish settlement. This checkpoint is classified in Hebrew as a *machsom seger* ('closure checkpoint'), or 'terminal', because it traverses an official boundary between Israel and the West Bank. I decided to live near this checkpoint since my fellowship at the Van Leer Institute required me to commute several times a week from Bethlehem to Jerusalem. Although as an American I remained shielded from much of the brutality that Palestinian workers regularly face, this experience did introduce me to their arduous commute, to the arbitrary detentions that made their lives hell, and to the pain of waiting for hours on end, not knowing whether you would ever reach your destination.

Hundreds of 'envelope checkpoints' (*machsom keder*), bisect Palestinian territory.[7] These are also known as 'flying checkpoints', since they can be set up at any time and in just about any place, without warning. From January 2017 to June 2018, Israeli forces set up 4,924 flying checkpoints.[8] While there are eleven terminal checkpoints in the occupied Palestinian territories, like Checkpoint 300, flying checkpoints populate most roads linking major Palestinian cities, often skirting the wall.

Checkpoint 300 is an advanced and semi-high-tech checkpoint that creates 'the illusion of the occupation's end while maximizing and stabilizing its techniques and effects'.[9] Dividing Jerusalem from Bethlehem, this terminal checkpoint resembles a warehouse made of corrugated steel. During peak hours, the terminal is filled with thousands of Palestinians waiting to get to work. During non-peak hours, when fewer Palestinians are permitted to cross the border, its wide swaths of empty space are punctured by an atmosphere of endless waiting.

Although the terminal is large enough to house many thousands of passers-through, Checkpoint 300's most desirable aisles are closed to Palestinians, even during the busiest hours. Special lanes are reserved for foreign visitors exiting the occupied Palestinian territories – a feature that makes legible the racial and ethnic distinctions that undergird the occupation.

The checkpoint edifice itself, crafted from corrugated steel and topped by a watchtower that overlooks the building, is a model of purpose-built efficiency. The shadows of the watchtower eerily evoke the classical panopticon structure developed by utilitarian philosopher Jeremy Bentham. Bentham conceived of the panopticon as a means of enabling the observer to surveil an enclosed population without that population being able to see who is watching them. This eerie ubiquity of the jailor's gaze is reproduced everywhere in the architecture of occupation.

While obstructing movement, the checkpoint's turnstiles also convey the atmosphere of a rigidly organized occupation. However, notwithstanding the semblance of order that prevails in such terminals, which began to be constructed towards the end of 2005, there is little evidence that the checkpoints serve the purpose for which they were ostensibly built – that of 'minimizing the damage to Palestinian life'.[10] Terminal checkpoints are built for display, partly to intimidate, but also to normalize the occupation and expand the mechanisms of surveillance. Introducing a new technology of governance, the terminal asserts the absolute power of the occupier over the occupied. Its architectural form epitomizes the permanent state of emergency through which the Israeli state justifies the occupation.

At checkpoints like the Gilo terminal dividing Bethlehem from Jerusalem, foreigners are allowed to pass seamlessly and without close scrutiny. Meanwhile, Palestinians are often detained and interrogated. This inverts the usual practice at international borders, which typically grant to natives and permanent residents privileges denied to foreign visitors.[11] At the checkpoint, the foreigner, not the native, benefits from a halo of immunity. Meanwhile, Palestinians are denied basic rights, as the state attempts to reduce them to mere bearers of life. As Michael Foucault would say, they become biopolitical subjects through which the state attempts to put into place the conditions needed to perpetuate biological life without securing human freedom. Foucault's description of biopolitical power as that which aims 'to ensure, sustain, and multiply life, to put this life in order' captures a key dynamic of Israeli settler-colonial rule.[12]

The Israeli state seeks to keep Palestinians alive, at least provisionally, in order to maintain some semblance of compliance with international legal norms, even as it entrenches laws and systems that prevent Palestinians from flourishing and achieving their full potential. This is how biopolitical governance works: by controlling and commodifying human life. Soldiers are typically only given brief assignments in any particular location, to ensure that they do not form connections or build relationships with the native population. When Palestinians refuse to internalize the unwritten norms of Israeli governmentality at the checkpoint, they become a target population, subject to perpetual surveillance and discipline that builds on perceptions of racialized difference. From time to time, this intolerable status quo implodes, and the normalization of violence leads to war, as Israeli soldiers shoot to kill. Most of the time, the damage inflicted is less dramatic and becomes apparent only over time – including through the theft of time.

Palestinian-British filmmaker Farah Nabulsi's short film, *The Present* (2020), memorably illustrates the impact of the checkpoint regime on Palestinians' everyday lives. The film tells the story of a Palestinian man named Yusuf who resides in the West Bank, not far from a checkpoint. Yusuf decides to give his wife a new refrigerator as a gift for their wedding anniversary. The film opens on the day of their anniversary, which falls on a day when Yusuf does not have to go to work. However, in order to get the refrigerator for his wife, he still has to go to Jerusalem. Refrigerators are not sold anywhere in Palestine.

In an instance of life imitating art, the film was shot on the premises of Checkpoint 300, through which Yusuf must pass in order to get to Jerusalem. In shooting the film, Palestinian actor Salah Bakri had to enter the checkpoint at 3 a.m., just as Palestinian workers must do every day in order to make it to Jerusalem by the start of the work day. Nabulsi did not seek permission from the Israeli army to film their activities or checkpoints. As she reasoned later, 'If you are asking the IDF for permission to film that . . . you are asking an illegal occupier to film its illegal occupation.'[13] Yusuf passes much of the day waiting at checkpoints with his daughter on his journey to Jerusalem. His efforts to bring the refrigerator home, and the many barriers he faces to this seemingly simple act, produce a stark narrative about human dignity under occupation.

Since the refrigerator cannot fit through the turnstiles Palestinians are required to use when they pass through the checkpoint, Yusuf must ask permission from an Israeli soldier standing by to push it through the wide road created for the exclusive use of settlers and foreigners. The soldier refuses and insults Yusuf, refusing to bend the rules. Finally, Yusuf loses his temper and yells at the soldier, which puts his own life in danger. The soldier points a gun at him, ready to shoot. Then, suddenly, the camera shifts: Yusuf's daughter, who had been quietly observing the escalation into violence, calmly pushes the refrigerator across the border using the road that is forbidden for Palestinians to use. The soldier threatens to report the young girl to the authorities. Ultimately, father and daughter go on their way, exhausted by a long and arduous day, which should have been a simple shopping trip. Nabulsi's short but moving story of everyday dignity in a context of systematic humiliation under occupation was awarded the 2021 BAFTA (British Academy of Film and Television Arts) award for Best British Short Film, and was nominated for an Oscar for Best Live Action Short Film in the same year. Like *200 Meters*, *The Present* powerfully communicates the total immiseration within which many Palestinians are forced to pass their lives.

A third film, *Blacklisted* (2021), directed by Mohammed Almughanni, originally of Gaza, conveys the same sense of claustrophobia.[14] An unnamed Palestinian man based in the West Bank learns that his beloved girlfriend will be moving to Jerusalem for work and to be closer to her family. Her move in effect spells the end to their relationship, as he will not be able to obtain permission from the Israeli authorities to leave the West Bank. He is devastated. The rest of the film revolves around the extreme steps he takes in order to see her again. Since he cannot obtain a permit to exit the West Bank legally, he attempts to scale a wall in order to escape. He is discovered by the Israeli border guards, who arrest him, confiscate his phone, and interrogate him under the assumption that he is a terrorist. The man's silence through-out the interrogation is astonishing: he refuses to defend himself, to explain he is not a terrorist, or to state what really drove him to scale the wall and risk his life. His refusal to speak is the ulti-mate expression of the toll the occupation has taken on his humanity: silence is one of the few means at his disposal for pre-serving his dignity, even if it increases the chances that he will be identified as a terrorist by the Israeli authorities.

Omar (2013), by Nazareth-born Palestinian-Dutch film direc-tor Hany Abu-Assad, mirrors the plot of *Blacklisted* in certain crucial respects. In both films, a young Palestinian man finds his life horizons cut short by the Israeli occupation. Whereas, in *Blacklisted*, the Palestinian man ends up in prison due to his despair over lost love, in *Omar*, the protagonist takes part in the assassination of an Israeli soldier. He refuses to confess his crime to his jailors, however, and is tortured. In each of these four films, freedom for Palestinians is restricted through the mecha-nisms of bureaucratic regulation. These restrictions are assertions of power, dictating who has the prerogative to speak and who is forced to remain silent. At the same time, each of these films radiates a sense of Palestinian agency. Giving a central role to characters who refuse to give up, they remind us that the erasure of Palestine will never be accepted without resistance.

At Checkpoint 300, workers wait patiently, but with ever-mounting frustration. The lines of waiting workers multiply exponentially while the aisles remain closed. Workers are often late for work for reasons beyond their control, and yet they are punished by their employers for lateness as if it were their fault that they cannot predict when they will reach their workplaces. Over the course of a year of commuting back and forth between Bethlehem and Jerusalem, I observed the beginnings of a riot as the workers, tired of waiting in a queue that had remained motionless for the past hour, began to shout. Israeli soldiers mounted the platforms perched high above the ground, pointed their guns at the crowd, and yelled at them to shut up. Curiously, these orders were delivered in English, a language in which neither the majority of Palestinians waiting in line, nor the majority of soldiers tasked to police them, were fluent. Given the lack of any other shared language between Israelis and Palestinians, their use of English should not have surprised me.[15] Yet, from my vantage point, this recourse to a foreign yet global language also attested to the way in which this conflict is entangled in international geopolitics. The use of an alien tongue in place of a local one as a medium of communication between soldiers and civilians reinforced the uncanny atmosphere of occupation, at least from my outsider point of view. Although no one was killed or injured during this particular protest, Palestinian workers are regularly crushed to death while waiting at this and other checkpoints.[16]

During one particularly fraught morning rush hour, a vendor who collected meagre wages by selling tea and coffee near the checkpoint from dawn until early afternoon reminisced with me on the vagaries of his economic life. 'The days that are bad for the workers are good for my business', he said as we conversed in front of a motionless queue. 'When the workers have to wait for three, four, and five hours, then business booms.' Nigel Parsons and Mark Salter have observed similar dynamics during their fieldwork at checkpoints in the West Bank: local traders profit economically from the long lines of tired and frustrated Palestinian workers. Documenting the 'stalls offering clothes, kitchen equipment, toys and kebabs . . . taxi ranks organised on either side of a barrier . . . medical tents ministering to the old and infirm', just outside checkpoint terminals, the authors transcribe a revealing comment from one local Palestinian: 'in the rest of the world, civilization developed around water; here in the West Bank, it grows around checkpoints'.[17]

The expanding borders of the settler colonies bisecting the West Bank have generated a new political economy that keeps

Palestinians in confinement while expanding the control of the Israeli state. Palestinians who cannot leave the West Bank survive economically by selling goods at the borders of checkpoints. Such entrepreneurial trends are a means of resistance to the occupation; yet, as Palestinian media theorist Helga Tawil-Souri notes, they also have 'serious political limitations'.[18] Although they help Palestinians survive in the short term, checkpoint economies normalize the checkpoint's coercive modes of surveillance.

Further away from the Jerusalem border, deep within the occupied Palestinian territories, Israel continues to rely on so-called 'flying checkpoints' to act as a buffer around the settlements. These are provisional structures that are easily erected and rapidly erased. Far removed from the radar of official representation, they facilitate forms of corruption that more permanent and visible racializing checkpoints, such as Checkpoint 300, cannot openly permit. Checkpoints on the road from Nablus to Hebron, for example, are relocated on a daily basis. At these checkpoints, the targets are broader than workers who have to queue to reach their destinations. Palestinian children headed for schools, students bound for universities, people seeking medical help, and even family members hoping to visit their relatives 'clamber up and down sand embankments or across ditches to circumvent concrete slabs and soldiers, who sometimes shoot at them', as Israeli journalist Amira Hass has observed.[19] As the only Israeli journalist to live in the Occupied Territories, Hass is one of the few Israelis who have written about checkpoints from a vantage point that foregrounds their impact on Palestinians.

The welcome signs fronting major checkpoints across the West Bank whitewash the occupation with upbeat slogans directed at foreigners and settlers passing by, such as 'Peace be with You'. Some of these are in varnished pastels, and include photographs of idyllic places and greetings in Arabic and Hebrew block-letters. Others have a neon glow. Each sign rewrites the occupation as a tourist's idyll. Anthropologists Hagar Kotef and Merav Amir interpret such insignia of settler-colonial governmentality as demonstrations by the occupying regime that Palestinians 'passing through are visitors and not people who need to cross the checkpoint' in order to reach their homes.[20] These signs are directly aimed at tourists as a welcoming gesture, and indirectly at Palestinians as an alienating gesture. Such amnesiac settler-colonial narratives are characteristic of racializing checkpoints.

The high-tech roads bisecting the West Bank and built with the intention of facilitating movement between Israel and the settlements are closed to Palestinians. Due to these multiple kinds of closure and enclosure, journeys that would be completed within half an hour under normal conditions extend from morning until afternoon, and from afternoon until evening. The topography introduced by the wall imposes on those who live behind it the requirement to seek a permit from the Israeli military in order to reach the other side of their town, even to visit friends and family. This makes recreational travel impossible, and necessary travel increasingly difficult and subject to Israeli bureaucratic whim.

While the theft of Palestinian land has been widely documented, the theft of Palestinians' time by the checkpoint regime has been less thoroughly addressed. Time is more difficult to partition than space; but its removal is no less consequential, and the ability to control one's time is just as essential to human dignity. The theft of Palestinian time has occurred simultaneously with the Israeli state's revisions of Palestinian pasts: the Nakba – the catastrophic displacement of 700,000 Palestinians that made possible the founding of the state of Israel in 1948 – has been made eternally recurrent. Narratives of displacement from the 1940s and afterwards are folded into the present.

As Hass notes, 'Unlike land, which can be restored and replaced and rehabilitated, time lost – through the policy of closure – is lost forever.'[21] The theft of Palestinians' time by the checkpoint regime erases local memories even more thoroughly than does the physical usurpation of its territories. Even if confiscated Palestinians' lands are eventually restored to their original owners, the time that has been squandered over the course of Palestinians' cross-generational struggles to survive and to remember cannot be recuperated. The accumulated years lost to waiting at checkpoints on their way to work, school, and friends permanently shape consciousness.

Ghassan Kanafani's novella *Men in the Sun* (1962) chronicles these acts of erasure in visceral form. The novella tells of three Palestinian refugees who travel to Kuwait in search of work. They arrange to be smuggled into Kuwait by a Palestinian truck driver. Since they lack the permits and other papers that would enable them to travel publicly, they must do so in secret, hiding in the truck's empty water tank whenever they approach a border crossing. Their journey is fraught with danger. At the last crossing, just before they reach Kuwait, the driver is delayed at the checkpoint by a state bureaucrat with a penchant for joking. The refugees suffocate in the overheated water tank while they await the driver's return. After he crosses the border into Kuwait and opens the tank, the driver discovers the corpses of the refugees whom he was transporting, suffocated in the heat while the official cracked jokes at the checkpoint.

The concluding moments of the men's lives are rendered in oblique detail. The narrative focuses on the desert conditions that led to their death inside the empty water tank. With the lucidity of a poet immersed in desert landscapes, Kanafani writes: 'The lorry, a small world, black as night, made its way across the desert like a heavy drop of oil on a burning sheet of tin.'[22] Like an engine of death, the lorry travels 'over the burning earth, its engine roaring remorselessly'. This cluster of words recurs four times during the course of the journey, like an ominous refrain. Eventually, the Palestinian refugees die in silence, suffocated by the sun. Overcome by passivity and helplessness, they are literally roasted alive. While the men inside silently perish, the bureaucrats at the checkpoint joke among themselves. The death of these three refugees is a parable for the fate of the Palestinian people.

Kanafani's story was adapted for film in 1972 as *The Dupes* – a title underscoring the sense of betrayal and abandonment at the heart of the story. Unsurprisingly, the Egyptian director, Tawfiq Saleh, decided that he could not let the Palestinians die in silence. He needed to end the film with more dramatic tension than Kanafani's narrative contained. So the camera pans back and forth between the bureaucrats at the checkpoint, who tease the driver with innuendoes about his sex life, and the Palestinian men locked in the water tank and banging for help. The contrast between the desperate pounding of the dying men seeking release from the water tank and the careless bantering of the checkpoint bureaucrats makes even more palpable the fact that their deaths could have been avoided if the Israeli state had not been given free rein to make hundreds of thousands of Palestinians into refugees, or if their labour rights had been respected.

With Kanafani's story as a literary and cinematic precedent, the scene in *200 Meters*, in which Mustafa and his fellow Palestinians hide in the boot of a car while they are smuggled across the border into Israel, acquires even greater resonance. In both cases, the border is a miniscule construction that only appears menacing when viewed from the perspective of Palestinians who are denied passage across it. Fifty years after Kanafani introduced the image of the smuggled refugees into Palestinian literature, shockingly little has changed. Palestinian territory continues to undergo forced erasure by the State of Israel, with the complicity of international foreign policy and international law. Palestinian film and literature amply attest that this erasure has not accomplished its goal of silencing Palestinian voices. Yet the damage inflicted in the process of suppression is substantial and cannot be compensated for.

As this chapter has suggested, checkpoints are among the most effective instruments of occupation. As a mode of governance and a tool of population control, they are used with increasing frequency by states that aim to subjugate resistant populations. Yet it is not only in Israel and other settler-colonial regimes that checkpoints suppress the population's freedom. The role played by checkpoints in the realm of geopolitics is echoed in the realm of political debate by the IHRA definition of antisemitism: both dictate what can and cannot be said, not according to what is right or wrong, but according to who happens to be in power. Like checkpoints on the ground, separating families and destroying lives with layers of obstruction, checkpoints on free expression require our resistance and vigilance. The next time a person or institution advocates for banning certain expressions of solidarity, or implies that criticisms should not be made out of fear of causing offence, we who are on the outside of this – or any other – conflict must refuse imposed silence. Our refusal is a way of resisting the physical barriers that stand in the way of Palestinian freedom. At present, our assent to censorship strengthens the state that keep these barriers in place.

2

Anti-Zionism before Israel

In 1967, an eventful year in Israel's relationship with the wider Middle East, Jewish Marxist Isaac Deutscher ominously described the role played by antisemitism in defining Jewish identity. 'It is a tragic and macabre truth that the greatest "re-definer" of the Jewish identity has been Hitler', Deutscher wrote. 'Auschwitz was the terrible cradle of the new Jewish consciousness and of the new Jewish nation.'[1] These words are taken from Deutscher's essay 'Who Is a Jew?' (begun in 1963, published posthumously in 1968). In this work, Deutscher both questions and asserts his Jewish identity. He acknowledges that, as an internationalist and atheist, he does not fit most conventional definitions of what makes a Jew. And yet there is another, arguably more fundamental sense in which Deutscher lays claim to being Jewish. 'I am, however, a Jew', he writes, 'by force of my unconditional solidarity with the persecuted and exterminated.' As someone who experienced the Jewish tragedy as his own, Deutscher wished to do all he could to assure 'the real, not spurious, security and self-respect of the Jews'.

For Deutscher, being a Jew is an exercise in negation. It is an identity that is formed against and in spite of the forces one opposes, as perhaps all identities are. Deutscher describes himself, and all twentieth-century Jews, as members of the 'negative community', comprising those who, repeatedly throughout history, have 'been singled out for persecution and extermination'. The negativity of Jewish identity is part of the fateful legacy it imposes on the life trajectory of every individual Jew. Although

Deutscher's Jewish identity is negative in the sense that it is framed in opposition to something else, the negative force of the Jewish tradition that includes such luminaries as Spinoza, Marx, Rosa Luxembourg, Trotsky, and Freud is also part of its creative offering. To say that Jewish identity is negative is not to criticize or condemn it, but to account for its persistence in historical terms. For 'non-Jewish Jews' like Deutscher, who operate within a Jewish intellectual tradition while rejecting the Jewish religion, Jewish identity exists only in the form of a negation.

As someone whose father died in Auschwitz, Deutscher was sympathetic to the concept of Israel, a state that he hoped would be a safe haven for Jews in the aftermath of the Holocaust. He disavowed his own anti-Zionism in 1954, which he said had been 'based on a confidence in the European labour movement, or, more broadly, in European society and civilisation, which that society and civilisation have not justified'.[2] Yet, as the occupation of Palestine persisted and displaced Palestinians continued to be barred from returning to their homes, Deutscher became more critical of the Israeli state. His harsh words for Israel are often suppressed by those eager to incorporate his legacy into a Zionist narrative.

Deutscher's late essays powerfully condemn all nationalisms, for Jews and for humanity in general. In his last interview, given to the *New Left Review* in 1967, just a few months before his death, Deutscher was sharply critical of Israel's policies towards its Palestinian population. 'The Arabs', he notes, 'were made to pay the price for the crimes the West committed towards the Jews. They are still made to pay it, for the "guilty conscience" of the West is, of course, pro-Israeli and anti-Arab.'[3] Deutscher predicted that the 1967 war Israel had recently won, prevailing over Egypt and the rest of the Arab world with disastrous consequences for Palestinians, would someday be seen 'in a not very remote future, to have been a disaster in the first instance for Israel itself'.[4] As for Israeli Jews, in the wake of the 1967 war they had become 'agents of the late, over-ripe, imperialist capitalism of our days'.[5] We will see that Deutscher's warnings were to prove prescient. Deutscher grasped the depth and horror of anti-semitism while also refusing to sentimentalize it or use it as a pretext for other injustices.

In the past as in the present, the search for Jewish identity is inseparable from antisemitism's legacy. The space for debating the issues Deutscher raised has shrunk dramatically during the past few decades. Many factors have contributed to this narrowing, including the ongoing dispossession of the Palestinian people and Israel's efforts to conceal these processes from the world. The promotion of new definitions of antisemitism that stigmatize, and in some cases criminalize, criticism of Israel has been a major part of this strategy. In this chapter, I show how the longer tradition of Jewish radicalism, which long pre-dates Zionism, can help to reframe the debate around antisemitism and contextualize it within a wider-ranging critique of capitalism that also compels us to rethink the relationship between the freedom to dissent and social equality.

When it comes to fighting antisemitism or any other racism, definitions are of limited use. The binary logic of definitions reduces all positions to either X or Y. According to this logic, either one is a Zionist (X) or an anti-Zionist (Y). There is no space in between. XY does not exist. Anti-Zionism is either the worst kind of antisemitism (if you are X) or the highest ethical duty of every human being (if you are Y). There is no room for ambiguity, and very little space for recognizing or accommodating the hybrid identities that so many of us inhabit. The binary logic of the discourse around antisemitism is a feature of our contemporary moment, and it has caused great harm to Jews and Palestinians. It is a symptom of the occupation of Palestine and the perpetual erasure of this political reality, rather than a step towards a solution.

Although the binary logic of definitions has not been helpful in eradicating antisemitism, it has been useful for those who seek to suppress criticism of Israel. Definition-based logic has a unique propensity to stifle freedom of expression, since labelling a certain view or statement antisemitic is a convenient way of stigmatizing it. This definition-based approach has contributed to the silencing of points of view that are critical of Israel, the censorship of pro-Palestinian voices, and the redirection of the world's attention away from Israel's occupation of Palestine. Instead of focusing on Palestinian rights, the media has been sucked into a toxic debate around antisemitism's competing definitions, trapping viewers in defensive postures and encouraging the application of double standards around Israel. The binary logic of definitions has been interrogated from many angles during the past fifteen years, but all of its manifestations have resulted in the same paralysis. The impact of this definitional logic, and the way out of our present paralysis, is the main focus of this chapter. Whether it is the IHRA definition that we oppose or the more open-ended Jerusalem Declaration that we advocate, all of these attempts to 'name' antisemitism are susceptible to abuse and misappropriation.

Although twenty-first-century debates around the definition of antisemitism have been contentious, they belong to a much longer tradition of controversy around the history of Jewish identity and Jew-hatred. Antisemitism has never been stable or singular in its operations. When the term *Antisemitismus* was popularized in 1879, with the publication of *The Triumph of Judaism over Germanism* by German publicist Wilhelm Marr, as a way of codifying different forms of Jew-hatred, it had been around as a concept for much longer.[6] Marr was of the view that antisemitism was a good thing. He wanted to encourage his fellow Jew-haters to identify themselves openly and to celebrate their animosity towards the Jewish minority, whom he saw as a stain on bourgeois Germany. Far from being a source of shame, being an antisemite was for Marr and many of his compatriots a badge of pride.

Marr popularized 'antisemitism' as a term, but he did not invent it. Try comparing the Christian Jew-hatred that predominated in the European Middle Ages with the blood-libel myth of the nine-teenth century or the pogroms that followed when Jews throughout Russia and Eastern Europe were accused of killing and eating children for the religious rituals. Such juxtapositions show us that, although certain motifs and themes persist over time, they rapidly adopt new forms and guises. Every new man-ifestation of antisemitism inevitably bears the imprint of its times. The diversity of Jew-hatred across time and space has imposed a huge burden on any effort to organize these manifes-tations of hate within a single framework or rubric, let alone to encompass them in a single term.

To borrow a phrase from philosopher Walter Bryce Gallie, antisemitism is an 'essentially contested term', like Judaism itself, if in a different sense. Attempts to ascribe to it a single meaning flounder against the reality of its multiplicity. Since antisemitism has never been stable, we should not be surprised to see its definition shift yet again in the twenty-first century, as it absorbs the changed circumstances of Jews and of Israel. What is more surprising is how uncritically and rapidly twenty-first-century definitions that focus predominantly on Israel and anti-Zionism as manifestations of antisemitism have been accepted and internalized within liberal Euro-American con-sciousness. These definitions have been remarkably successful at shutting down debate, rather than opening it to wider hori-zons. Few of those with the authority and power to determine which definitions are adopted and how they are implemented have seriously reflected on the consequences of their choices. Never has Deutscher's observation that Palestinians have been made to pay for the guilty conscience of the West been more applicable. How were antisemitism and anti-Zionism conceived and debated before the founding of the state of Israel? The remainder of this chapter addresses this question by considering how Jews conceived of their predicament before the founding of Israel shifted political alliances and brought us to our current impasse.

Notwithstanding efforts by contemporary supporters of Israel to associate anti-Zionism with antisemitism, scepticism towards the idea of a Jewish nation-state has a long history within Judaism, and not only on the left. An opinion piece published in 1916 in the London-based Yiddish radical newspaper *Worker's Friend* (*Arbeter Fraynd*) warned of the dangers that establishing a homeland would present for Jews around the world, and insisted on a different approach to the problem of antisemitism. Antisemitism would only cease to exist, the authors argued, 'in a society in which the oppressed are united against the oppressors'.[7] The *Worker's Friend* was the mouthpiece of a Yiddish-speaking anarchist collective based in London's East End that organized lectures and classes in history, sociology, and literature. This group was also involved in a number of garment workers' strikes, including one that lasted for three weeks in 1906. The circle that read and contributed to *Worker's Friend* was opposed to the establishment of a single state for the Jewish people because, as the editorial continued, 'the struggle for Jewish national rights – even if successful – will only lead to the establishment of a Jewish state under the domination of the Jewish bourgeoisie'.

Unfortunately for the anti-Zionist movement, *Worker's Friend* was suppressed by the British government amid the tensions of World War I. Although members of this collective would later influence communist movements around the world, their impact on the cultural and intellectual life of British Jewry was cut short by the war, as well as by internal shifts within the British Jewish community towards Zionism. When Rudolf Rocker, the non-Jewish German anarchist editor of *Worker's Friend*, was arrested in 1918 for opposing both sides in the war and deported to the Netherlands, this effectively meant the end of *Worker's Friend* as a venue for the expression of anti-Zionist points of view. Although British anti-Zionism persisted among left-leaning Jews, the closure of such newspapers inaugurated a demographic shift both within British Jewry and on the left.

In 1917, after years of internal deliberation and negotiations between the British cabinet and the Zionist Organization, foreign secretary Lord Arthur James Balfour penned the famous letter that came to be called the Balfour Declaration. Speaking on behalf of the British government, Balfour announced that it favoured 'the establishment in Palestine of a national home for the Jewish people' and would 'use [its] best endeavours to facilitate the achievement of this object'. Balfour's second clause, noting that 'nothing shall be done which may prejudice the civil and religious rights of existing non-Jewish communities in Palestine', has been forgotten in theory and neglected in practice.

Although the sixty-seven-word sentence that comprises the Balfour Declaration of 1917 was even more consequential than the thirty-eight words of the IHRA definition adopted by the British government one hundred years later, the parallels between the two documents are striking. Both adoptions reflect a dangerous tendency on the part of an imperial power to homogenize a heterogenous constituency, to ignore dissenting voices within that homogenized collective, and to subordinate minority rights to political exigency. Finally, both documents acquired popularity, and even a certain kind of authority, less as a way of fighting antisemitism than of displacing it. In the case of the first document, the rights of an entire people, the Palestinians, were erased in order to accommodate Britain's wartime strategy. In the case of the second document, the accusation of antisemitism was used as a weapon to conceal more than a century of imperial complicity.

It has been argued that the entire Balfour Declaration was based on a misunderstanding – or, rather, on a series of miscalculations. Historian Mark Levene has identified three mistakes made by the British Foreign Office at the outbreak of World War I which caused them to commit to creating a Jewish homeland in Palestine:

1. The Jews were a collective entity.
2. The Jews were powerful.
3. The Jews were pro-German.[8]

Among the primary strategic objectives of the war cabinet during World War I was to ensure that Jews sided with the entente – the alliance comprising Britain and its wartime ally Russia – against Germany. Showing support for Zionism appeared to be the surest way of gaining political leverage with Jews around the world. Redrawing the map of a Middle Eastern geography seemed like a small price to pay if it ensured that Jews would support Britain during the war. These calculations were based on an exaggerated view of Jews' political power and an unrealistic perception of their loyalty to Germany. In his own words, then prime minister David Lloyd George believed that promising 'the fulfilment of Zionist aims in Palestine' would 'bring Russian Jewry to the cause of the Entente'.[9]

Responses among Britain's Jewish community to the Balfour Declaration were divided, but it definitely marked a sea change in British–Jewish relations, as well as internally within British Jewry. In the pages of the *Jewish Chronicle*, Zionist leaders Chaim Weizmann, Nachum Sokolow, and Yechiel Tschlenow published a joint 'Zionist Manifesto' under the aegis of the London Bureau of the Zionist Organization.[10] Their manifesto set the tone for how the Balfour Declaration would be interpreted by subsequent generations, including which parts would be remembered and which parts forgotten.

Even though the British government did not accede to their every wish, the Zionist negotiators embraced the Balfour Declaration wholeheartedly. Needless to say, they recast the declaration in terms of their own political goals, which included the erasure of Palestinians. Boldly addressing their manifesto 'To the Jewish People', the authors called the Balfour Declaration 'an important milestone on the road to our national future'.[11] In their celebratory analysis, they reframed the way in which the Balfour Declaration would be read by subsequent generations. They used the occasion to call on all Jews to join the Zionist Organization in order to take advantage of this new opportunity to build a homeland in Palestine. From now on, they insisted, 'every gathering of Jews must have a practical aim, every speech must deal with a project, every thought must be a brick with which to build the National Home'. The authors of the *Jewish Chronicle* manifesto naively hoped that the Balfour Declaration would put an end to internal Jewish dissent around Palestine and Jewish emigration. Yet dissent around the establishment of the state of Israel never disappeared. The objections of early-twentieth-century anti-Zionist Jews resonate to this day.

In keeping with their directive to turn every speech into a political project, the authors politicized the Balfour Declaration even beyond its original content. Their interpretation omits Balfour's caveat that, in recognizing Palestine as the Jewish homeland, nothing should be done to endanger 'the civil and religious rights of existing non-Jewish communities in Palestine'. This caveat had been secured by anti-Zionist Jews with connections to the government, who had expressed concern over the 'proposal to give to the Jews of Palestine privileges not shared by the rest of the population of that country'.[12] Balfour proceeded regardless of their fears, but he did offer the concession of promising not to infringe on the rights of 'non-Jewish communities'. This was not quite the same as recognizing Palestinian rights, but under different circumstances, and given different geopolitical alignments, it might have made a difference. Like the IHRA definition, the document was instrumentalized in the most cynical way. Predictably, the authors of the 'Zionist Manifesto' had nothing to say about Balfour's caveat. They saw in the text only 'an official promise of support and help in the realization of our ideal of liberty in Palestine', and forgot about the rest.

Lord Balfour's caveat about not undermining the rights of existing non-Jewish communities was a concession to the Conjoint Foreign Committee (CFC), whose outspoken opposition to Zionism was already noted. This organization was founded in 1878 with the aim of representing Jewish interests in international politics. Led by diplomat and journalist Lucian Wolf, the CFC's influence persisted during the negotiations that culminated in the Balfour Declaration. Even though their aims were overridden by the Zionist faction, they were regarded as a '"shadow foreign office" of Anglo-Jewry'.[13] While leaders of the Zionist Organization were busy lobbying the British government to set up a homeland for the Jews in Palestine, the CFC focused on bringing about legal equality for the world's Jewry, particularly in Russia, where until recently Jews had been legally segregated from the rest of the population and compelled to reside in the Pale of Settlement. As a Foreign Office record of a meeting with Wolf noted, more 'stress [was] laid on the emancipation of Russian Jews than on the Palestine question'.[14]

Wolf and the CFC expressed at most qualified support for the idea of a Jewish homeland. Specifically, they pointed to the need to protect the rights of the local Arab population in Palestine.[15] But the most significant and strenuous objections to the Balfour Declaration came from another source: Edwin Montagu, British secretary of state for India from 1917 to 1922, and the third practising Jew ever to serve in the British cabinet. Montagu was openly hostile to the British government's attempt to placate Zionists by creating a homeland for the Jews in Palestine. When a draft copy of what would become the Balfour Declaration fell into Montagu's hands, he drafted a five-page memo provocatively entitled 'The Anti-Semitism of the Present Government'. At the time, this document was among the most powerful diagnoses and indictments of the settler-colonial mentality that continues to link the contemporary state of Israel to Britain's imperial legacy.

Montagu's prediction of the impact of the Balfour Declaration was prescient. 'When the Jew has a national home surely it follows that the impetus to deprive [him] of the rights of British citizenship must be enormously increased', he wrote; 'Palestine will become the world's Ghetto.'[16] While the first part of this prediction has arguably not come to pass, Montagu's foreboding that Palestine would become the world's ghetto has been realized, in ways that even Montagu may not have expected. How, he asked the government, could he negotiate for British government interests in India if that very government regarded him as a transitory resident, whose actual homeland was in Palestine? When he was informed by the government that the declaration had been finalized, Montagu recorded in his diary: 'The Government has dealt an irreparable blow to Jewish Britons, and they have endeavoured to set up a people which does not exist.'

From a contemporary perspective, Montagu's statements are open to criticism. At moments, he appears to accept antisemitism as reasonable. He states, for instance, that he has no desire 'to deny that anti-Semitism can be held by rational men'. Such outmoded sentiments were expressed by all sides, including the Zionist Organization. Reflecting on these proceedings several decades later, Harry Sachar, a board member of the World Zionist Organization, wrote of the British political class of the time that it had 'a residual belief in the power and the unity of Jewry'.[17] This prejudice, he added, causes Jews to suffer, 'but it is not wholly without its compensations'. In a troubling statement that portends Israel's subsequent role in world politics, Sachar notes that this prejudice 'plays, consciously or unconsciously, its part in the calculations and the decisions of statesmen. To exploit it delicately and deftly belongs to the art of the Jewish diplomat.'

As we have seen, the conflicts between Zionists and anti-Zionists during the years leading up to and immediately following the issuance of the Balfour Declaration in 1917 bear uncanny similarities to the controversies around the IHRA definition during the first decades of the twenty-first century. In both historical junctures, Jewish interests were often reduced to political instruments, and Jews became proxies for achieving other agendas. Governments and public institutions favoured certain demands at certain times in order to advance political goals unrelated to Jewish equality. In both moments, too, political exigency trumped moral probity. Just as right-wing Christian fundamentalists are among the most vocal supporters of the state of Israel during the twenty-first century, so were many non-Jewish politicians who aligned with the Zionist cause themselves anti-semites. Anti-Zionist intellectual Claude Joseph Montefiore, who headed the Anglo-Jewish Committee and was also involved the CFC, understood this well. As he wrote in 1916 in the *Fortnightly Review*, 'All anti-Semites are enthusiastic Zionists.'[18]

The origins of the Balfour declaration should be traced not to 'the wartime policies and strategies of Britain in the Middle East', but rather to 'the murky waters of modern anti-Semitism'.[19] This analysis can also be applied to the political climate that led to the adoption of the IHRA definition one hundred years later by the same country that had ceded Palestine to Zionist Jews through the Balfour Declaration – an event that British historian Elizabeth Monroe has judged 'one of the greatest mistakes in our imperial history'.[20] Among the countries that were the first to adopt the definition was Hungary, which would chair the IHRA in 2015 and 2016, when the momentum behind the IHRA definition was at its peak. Although nearly all European countries have a dark and entangled relationship with antisemitism, Hungary is distinct for its persistent denial of its role in the Holocaust and for the ongoing popularity of its antisemitic right-wing political parties, such as Jobbik. These antisemitic links did not prevent Hungary from playing a leading role in disseminating the IHRA definition and proposing its adoption. Nor did similar issues prevent Romania, well known for its role in the Romani genocide of 1935–45, from also assuming a prominent position within this organization. The examples of Hungary and Romania are notable not simply for their histories of antisemitism and ethnic cleansing; they are also relevant for understanding the political uses of antisemitism today. These histories continue to be suppressed and unacknowledged in the countries where they occurred, even while those countries are allowed to chair the IHRA, hence becoming honorary stewards of the IHRA definition.

Lord Balfour's cousin Robert Cecil, a diplomat best known as one of the main architects of the League of Nations, offered an antisemitic assessment on a Foreign Office document that speaks for the overall attitude of the government he represented: 'I do not think it is possible to exaggerate the international power of the Jews.'[21] This same Cecil argued for rapprochement with the Jews on distinctively antisemitic grounds. 'It is most regrettable that in view of the vast financial influence of the Jews, the Russians make so little effort to conciliate them', he wrote in 1916, while parliamentary under-secretary at the Foreign Office.[22] Antisemitism like Cecil's was a significant factor in British politics, including in the decision to support Zionist Jews in their efforts to claim Palestine as their homeland. British politicians feared that, if they did not support the Zionist cause, Jews would align with the Germans during World War I.[23]

Montefiore's assessment of the relation between Zionism and antisemitism applies to the current political landscape just as much as it did to the Zionist movement of the early twentieth century. The twentieth-century antisemites who drafted the Balfour Declaration did so at least partly because of their exaggerated fears of Jewish influence in world politics. Like their compatriots in the following century, 'the protagonists of the Balfour Declaration heard only what they wanted to hear'.[24] Their embrace of Zionism did not mitigate or undermine their deeply rooted antisemitism. Nor did it prevent other branches of that same government from seeking to deport all Russian Jews of military age who had refused to fight in the war. It was even proposed in 1918, a year after the Balfour Declaration, that these dissenting Jews be sent to 'concentration camps' prior to their deportation.[25] The words 'concentration camps' had rather different and less sinister connotations in 1918 than they would in 1938, but the brutality of British colonialism towards those perceived as civilizationally inferior was on full display by this date. The British government's willingness to hand over Palestine to Zionist Jews thus hardly seems like an act of solidarity or friendship. It was a crude political calculation, and a mistaken one at that. What is most tragic is that the same political mistakes that were made in 1917 continue to be made one hundred years later, in connection with the IHRA definition and the international community's willingness to accommodate it to Israel's annexation of Palestinian lands.

The weaponization of fundamental rights that we witness today in connection with the IHRA definition, combined with obliviousness and indifference to Palestinian prerogatives, is in many respects a continuation of nineteenth-century European colonial power relations. Then as now, dissenters were suppressed when their criticisms undermined the expansionist aims of the state. Such is the lesson of the Balfour Declaration today.

European antisemitism has had impacts on communities that played no part in its creation, most notably Palestinians. The history of anti-Zionism before the establishment of the State of Israel illuminates dynamics that emerged after 1948. From this vantage point, the IHRA definition itself appears as simply the latest realignment of imperial rule with geopolitics. These imperial legacies also underwrite Israeli settler-colonialism. Yet, whereas during the nineteenth century the British Empire had no qualms about broadcasting its imperial designs on the Holy Land and aligning with Zionism, in the twenty-first century multicultural liberal states attempt to maintain a pretence of neutrality when arbitrating between Israel and Palestine. The right-wing weaponization of free speech further exacerbates this situation, making unsayable the common sense of prior eras. The balance of power continues to be aligned against Jews and Palestinians alike. The IHRA definition, like the Balfour Declaration before it, has thereby become a means of papering over the entrenched structural inequalities that underwrite contemporary imperialism.

Instead of inducing despair, this historical legacy can become a resource for resistance. We can also probe the untapped potential of radical socialist approaches to the liberation of Jews and Palestinians within a broader framework of human emancipation. Around the end of the nineteenth century and the beginning of the twentieth century, Jews began to develop powerful critiques of colonialism that incorporated the history of anti-semitism into their understanding of power.

Although the Zionist account of antisemitism that is opposed to Jewish assimilation is most prevalent today, the economic critique of antisemitism has uncovered many aspects of Jewish history that remain relevant, both in the struggle against anti-semitism and in efforts to resist the weaponization of this struggle by pro-Israel advocates. This economic critique can be traced to the early writings of Karl Marx, but it by no means ended with him. Over the course of a century, Marxist Jewish thought developed and refined Marx's controversial initial insights into the relationship between Jews and capitalism.

This book has been written in the belief that there is a way out of our present censorious malaise. Much of the path for that exit – and the prospects for a better future – was furnished by Jewish Marxists from prior decades who were critical of Zionism. Nor did they stop with a critique of the Zionist project. Early-twentieth-century revolutionaries like Leon Trotsky (1879–1940) and Abram Leon (1918–44) situated the persecution of the Jewish people within a longer history of capitalist exploitation, arguing that, as Trotsky wrote in 1940, 'the salvation of the Jewish people is bound up inseparably with the overthrow of the capitalist system'.[26] In pursuit of an alternative approach to the critique of antisemitism, the next chapter explores mid-twentieth-century radical Jewish thinkers like Trotsky and Leon, whose critiques of antisemitism focused on political economy and economic history. Having so far considered the various diplomatic manoeuvres among early-twentieth-century Jews who were sceptical of Zionism, it is time to examine more closely the ideas that underwrote those activities. As Enzo Traverso, one of the most important contemporary chroniclers of radical Jewish thought, has argued, since 'Jewish socialism has been erased from the map of Europe', it is our responsibility 'to prevent it from being erased from history'.[27]

3

A Materialist Critique of Antisemitism: Introducing Abram Leon

Among the outstanding contributors to the Jewish Marxist critique of antisemitism are the Russian revolutionary Leon Trotsky and his follower from Belgium Abram Leon. As Trotsky's main biographer in English, Isaac Deutscher, whose literary legacy spans the period between World War II and the Israeli Six-Day War of 1967, belongs to this same tradition. The lives of each of these thinkers were profoundly shaped by wartime conditions, which tested and refined their convictions. Many other left-leaning Jewish thinkers wrote about antisemitism during these same years. Hannah Arendt (1906–75), whose early work in German on antisemitism makes an important if under-examined contribution to the debate, also belongs to this group, as does Walter Benjamin (1892–1940), who developed a messianic materialism that both engaged with and transcended the Marxist critique.[1] I focus here on Leon and Trotsky because they were specifically concerned with the critique of antisemitism from a radical Marxist perspective, and incorporated this critique into their anti-capitalist worldviews. For Leon and Trotsky, the critique of antisemitism was an extension of the Marxist critique of capitalism's political economy, adapted for a fascist age.

Leon's and Trotsky's critiques of antisemitism were developed during the Nazi assault on Europe, at a time when the Jewish people were faced with the existential threat of genocide. These circumstances meant that their ideas were tested under extreme conditions, stripped of any illusions about human nature.

Remarkably, the extraordinary pressures under which they laboured did not lead them to compromise their positions. Far from rendering it obsolete, the genocide of the Jewish people sharpened their analysis and deepened their critiques of Zionism. Their approaches to antisemitism remain as intersectional, as cosmopolitan, as grounded in political economy, and ultimately as relevant to our political present as they were in their inception. The materialist critique of antisemitism has been overshadowed by other approaches, and has fallen out of fashion along with many other Marxist critiques. Yet the materialist critique has a great deal to offer those who wish to reframe the debate around the IHRA definition, and to move beyond clashes over nominalist definitions.

Leon developed Trotsky's scattered insights into a full-fledged theory of antisemitism that also entailed a detailed understanding of the socioeconomic role of the Jewish people throughout history. According to Leon (following Trotsky, who took his cue from Marx), the origin of anti-Jewish racism is best revealed through a materialist account of transformations in the political economy. The religious identity of the Jewish people masked their even more salient economic roles as merchants, tradespeople, and brokers between the ruling class and the peasantry. Engaging with this history, Leon developed a sociological theory of Jews as a 'people-class', somewhat analogous to Weber's account of Jews as a pariah people. Leon's theory of the 'people-class' has been criticized by later scholars as an oversimplification, but the term itself is not central to his argument.[2] It is entirely possible to reject the label of 'people-class' while still benefiting from Leon's socioeconomic insights, and concurring with his visionary understanding of antisemitism as 'the dialectical product of Western civilization'.[3]

Leon has also been criticized for his economic determinism and his inaccurate assumption that Jews were, in all times and places throughout history, primarily – or even exclusively – involved in mercantile activity. Yet, as David Ruben has argued,

'Leon's thesis could be stated in such a way as to make it compat-
ible with almost unlimited evidence about occupational difference
within Jewries, as long as one could always find evidence of
some group of Jews engaging in exchange-related occupations
within each Jewry'.[4] In other words, it is enough to establish that
some – even if not most – Jews were consistently engaged in
exchange-related occupations throughout history to demonstrate
the relevance of Leon's arguments about Jews in relation to
capitalism. Leon certainly overstates the empirical evidence that
supports his theory, but his impassioned tone, which can easily
be read as a product of his fraught environment and of the everyday stress imposed by the Nazi occupation, does not require that
we reject the theory itself.

Sympathetic readers of Leon like John Rose have suggested
the term 'merchant class' in lieu of 'people-class' as the category
by which we should understand the socioeconomic role of the Jews
throughout history.[5] 'Merchant class' may well be an improve-
ment on 'people-class', because it is more concretely rooted in a
recognizable form of economic activity. What remains of value
is Leon's insistence on interrogating antisemitism through the
lens of the political economy. This approach was revolutionary
in 1942, when the book was written, and remains so today. The
key shift that contributed to the rise of modern antisemitism
was away from feudalism, under which Jews financed the lavish
lifestyles of the nobility and made possible the military expedi-
tions of kings, towards capitalism, which made traditional Jewish
social functions obsolete. By engaging with Leon's account of
the origins of antisemitism – and delving deep into the socioeconomic origins of antisemitism – we can generate a materialist
framework for the critique of antisemitism that will render
obsolete nominalist definitions like that of the IHRA, as well
as provisional and necessarily incomplete solutions like that of
the JDA.

Leon's Jewish Questions

On 2 November 1917, the British foreign secretary, Arthur Balfour, penned a public letter to Lord Rothschild, an entrepreneur who regarded himself as a leader of the Anglo-Jewish community. As publicized by the press a week later, the letter proclaimed that the British government would support 'the establishment in Palestine of a national home for the Jewish people'. The significance of the IHRA definition of antisemitism in the twenty-first century, much like that of the Balfour Declaration, is difficult to perceive from the document itself. The importance of the Balfour Declaration for Palestinian and Jewish history derives from the ways in which the promises made by Balfour, on no authority other than that granted by his colonial mentality, were implemented in subsequent decades.

The resistance to the Balfour Declaration among early-twentieth-century British Jews set the stage for subsequent anti-Zionist initiatives, which were often led by Jews who had come of age within a revolutionary leftist tradition that viewed Zionism as a progressive movement for national liberation from an imperial yoke. Abram Leon, Isaac Deutscher, and Hannah Arendt all fit this biographical trajectory. Each began their intellectual journeys as committed Zionists, even though they eventually broke with this tradition and became Zionism's harshest critics. As a result of their early involvement with the Zionist movement, each understood Zionism from within. While the circle around the Yiddish *Worker's Friend* was among the earliest manifestations of Jewish anti-Zionism, this opposition persisted, through the most difficult years of persecution for Jews under Nazi occupation, and even in the wake of the Holocaust, to develop into a robust philosophical creed.

Leon was the torchbearer of Marxist anti-Zionism during World War II. Although he managed in his brief life to offer a strikingly original account of how capitalist economies fostered antisemitism, he was unable to see his work through to publication, as he did not survive the Nazi genocide. Nonetheless, he managed to do what no one else had adequately done before him: develop Marx's insights concerning the relationship between Jews and capitalism, while also significantly revising the flawed conflation of Jews with capitalism that we find in the early Marx. In its place, we find a more compelling and nuanced account of how the decline of Jewry and the rise of antisemitism were fostered by the capitalist world economy.

Leon was born in Warsaw under the traditional Jewish name Abraham Wejnstok. In the absence of extant biographical material about Abram Leon to explain why he chose the name by which he is better known, we can speculate that it was in homage to Trotsky that Abraham Wejnstok chose to adopt the name 'Leon' once he became politically active.[6] Zionist sentiment among his middle-class family was so intense that they briefly migrated to Palestine when Leon was still a child in grammar school. The family returned to Europe within a year, and moved to Belgium in 1926, where Leon grew up. He briefly became a prominent member of the local left-wing Zionist organization, the Young Guard (Hashomer Hatzair). However, Leon soon detected two fatal flaws in the Zionist project, which made it incompatible with his revolutionary ambitions. The first was the nationalism that underwrote the Zionist agenda, which it had internalized from European history. The second was its uncritical embrace of capitalist ideology, which ultimately contributed to the destruction of Jewry, as he explains in his book.

Having rejected Zionism, Leon embraced Trotsky's version of Marxism after hearing the fiery speeches of political activist Walter Dauge, founder of the Revolutionary Socialist Party, to Belgian coalminers. Leon consistently distinguished between the Marxist movement to which he committed all of his energies and the Soviet state that had in his view perverted and undermined Marxist values with its own brand of fascism. The clarity of his political vision, combined with the arduous conditions he faced, enabled him to see through the hypocrisies and limitations of his contemporaries, and to develop an incisive account of the relation between capitalism and antisemitism in Jewish history.

Leon's political talents became evident to the world when, following Trotsky's assassination in Mexico in 1940 by Stalin's henchmen, he founded Belgium's first Trotskyist political party. He also became editor-in-chief of *Lenin's Way* (*La Voie de Lénine*, 1941–45), and the primary contributor to this newspaper, which he managed to publish during even the most difficult days of the Nazi occupation. *Lenin's Way* was distributed through underground networks, as it could not legally be published in occupied Belgium. The physical format of the newspaper's issues from 1941 to 1945 reveals a gradual deterioration of working conditions.[7] Paper grew scarcer with every issue, and professional printers were forced to shut down. The newspaper was issued in increasingly brief instalments, using widely varying typefaces and page design. In spite of all the challenges he faced, Leon never ceased his work as an editor, writer, and activist, up until the day of his arrest.

The revolutionary movement to which Leon belonged was hopeful that the defeat of Benito Mussolini during 1943–44 augured the defeat of fascism. When the Allies landed in Normandy, the war seemed to be over and the defeat of fascism seemed certain. Hopeful of peace, Leon emerged from his underground existence and travelled openly to the Belgian city of Charleroi, where he hoped to settle permanently. Charleroi had become a centre for miners who were active in the revolutionary workers' movement, and Leon wanted to support their organizing activities. He was arrested by the Gestapo on the very night of his arrival in Charleroi and taken to prison, where he was tortured. Leon's skills in underground organizing served him well during his imprisonment; he smuggled out letters and managed to establish contact with the party leadership. Although his magnum opus survived in the notebooks that he had left behind at the time of his arrest, and was published two years after his death, Leon himself died in the gas chambers of Auschwitz at the young age of twenty-six.

The notebooks in which he had composed *The Jewish Question* were miraculously preserved by Leon's friends, who managed to publish the book in France soon after the war. This first edition was accompanied by a biographical sketch from Leon's friend, comrade, and fellow revolutionary Ernest Mandel (writing under the pseudonym E. Germain). Although the first edition was translated into Portuguese, English, and Spanish during the 1940s and 1950s, the book was forgotten soon thereafter. The work's thorough critique of Zionism, which included an indictment of antisemitism before Hitler, was too visionary for its time. The book only attained the fame it deserved during the 1960s, following the Six-Day War, during which Israel annexed East Jerusalem, and the very existence of the Jewish state became a defining question in leftist debates. During these years, *The Jewish Question* was published in Spanish, Arabic, Swedish, German, and Japanese, as well as in thirteen different English-language editions.

What made Leon's book so exceptional? Ever since antisemitism had become a focus of inquiry and critique in modern Europe, there had been a tendency to conflate Jews with capitalism. The class interests represented and promoted by these 'Jewish capitalists' were seen as hostile to the interests of the working class and the peasantry. Marx himself fell victim to this prejudice in his early essay 'On the Jewish Question' (1843), for which he has been criticized by later scholars of antisemitism.[8] Only occasionally is it recognized that Marx was arguing in this work against the even more demeaning associations between Jews and capitalists made by German philosopher Bruno Bauer. The trope of the Jew as the archetypal capitalist acquired even more grotesque form in Werner Sombart's *The Jews and Modern Capitalism* (1911), a popular work of socialist economic history. Leon criticizes Sombart for inverting the causal relationship between religion and class consciousness, and for allowing religion to function as an explanatory factor specifically in the case of the Jews.[9] As a leading socialist, Sombart would certainly have rejected the charge of antisemitism, had it been directed towards him. Yet Sombart is not alone among left-leaning thinkers in producing analyses of capitalism that turned Jews into symbols of capitalist accumulation while ignoring the ways in which capitalists have exploited Jews, banishing them to the margins of the social order.[10]

Leon intervened in this tradition by blowing apart the traditional association between Jews and the capitalist world order. In his view, this association had fuelled much antisemitism, past and present. In the process, Leon developed a materialist critique of capitalist exploitation that was wholly within the Marxian tradition. The perception that anti-capitalism and antisemitism are intertwined continues to shape the politics around the IHRA definition, and often drives attacks on leftist elements within the Labour Party. This has generated an atmosphere in which the critique of capitalism is sometimes dismissed as presumptively antisemitic. Even those who challenge the stereotypes generated by the intertwining of Jews and capitalism rarely contest it on empirical grounds. Leon's critique of the supposed alignment between capitalism and Jews undermined an entire strain of leftist antisemitism, thereby also undoing an entire tradition of right-wing attacks on socialism as inherently antisemitic.

Both antisemites and their opponents generally assume that Jews were beneficiaries of the capitalist system. As a result, the critique of antisemitism all too often becomes insulated from or even hostile to the critique of capitalism, while the critique of capitalism sometimes verges on antisemitism. Leon approaches Jews' relation to capitalism from a new angle, inverting the causal relation between the two. He translates into historical terms Trotsky's insistence that 'the Jewish question' could never be resolved 'within the framework of rotting capitalism and under the control of British imperialism'.[11] On his account, Jewry entered a period of decline with the advent of the capitalist world order, and antisemitism was one of the symptoms of this decline. Hence, far from being implicated in antisemitism, the critique of capitalism constitutes a first step in overcoming the economic exploitation of Jews and other oppressed and marginalized peoples. Although Leon's argument gained a following on the left during pivotal moments in Israeli and Palestinian history, his work has proved too radical to have received a coherent response – or even been properly absorbed – within mainstream Jewish studies.[12] Meanwhile, notwithstanding their many important critiques of Zionism as settler-colonialism, contemporary leftists have by and large failed to 'assess the history of the debate on the Jewish question inside the left'.[13]

The Jewish Question: A Marxist Interpretation is the title by which Leon's major work is known in many languages, including German, Spanish, and English. Yet the original French title reveals the author's methodology more effectively than do these translations. *La conception matérialiste de la question juive* can be translated as *The Materialist Interpretation of the Jewish Question*. While diverging from the original, the English version rightly emphasizes the link between Leon's work and its arguably most influential predecessor: Marx's essay 'On the Jewish Question' (1843). While Marx's early essay inaugurated a tradition in which Jewish history and the history of antisemitism were understood in light of their material conditions, Leon took Marx's methodology further than Marx himself did, making the method of materialist critique that he had learned from Marx serve genuinely anti-racist ends. As Tom Navon observes, Marxist Jewish historians like Leon share in common an 'unannounced rejection of young Marx's identification of Jews with modern capitalism', even as they develop and elaborate the incipient arguments of Marx's later work in relation to Jews and capitalist exploitation.[14]

Leon emulates Marx's method of combining sociological with political and economic analysis, and his citations from Marx's *Capital* shed new light on Marx's work, placing it in a distinctively Jewish framework. Although he does not name Trotsky as a source of inspiration anywhere in his book, readers familiar with Trotsky's approach to the Jewish question will instantly recognize his imprint. Trotsky's statement that 'capitalism took the Jewish people out of the ghetto and utilized them as an instrument in its commercial expansion' could have been written by Leon.[15] But, preoccupied as he was with the Russian revolution, Trotsky never offered a full-fledged account of the origins of antisemitism; that task was left to Leon. Leon also brought a deeper and more nuanced engagement with history to Trotsky's streamlined political analysis. Trotsky's example encouraged Leon to step out from under Marx's shadow, and to challenge the premises in Marx's early work. Leon grafted onto this powerful set of influences insights from more recent advances in the sociology of knowledge, including those of German sociologist Max Weber, to develop further the untapped potential of Marx's materialist paradigm.

Marx influenced Leon with his imagery as well as his argument. While explaining the fetishism of the commodity form, Marx remarked in *Capital* that 'trading nations, properly so called, exist in the ancient world only in its interstices, like the gods of Epicurus in the Intermundia, or like Jews in the pores of Polish society.'[16] This reference to the cosmology of the ancient Greek materialist philosopher Epicurus, on whom Marx had written his PhD thesis, was not fortuitous.[17] Epicurus held that the gods existed in the space between different cosmological systems, in a realm called Intermundia – literally, 'in between worlds' – and were unable to intervene in human affairs. This nod to theism aside, Epicurus, much like Marx, rejected the possibility of divine intervention. While this allusion to classical Greek mythology attested to Marx's erudition, it was also a covert – and, given that it came a quarter century after his first encounter with it, perhaps unconscious – reference to a similar comparison proposed by Bruno Bauer in the book that Marx had polemicized against in 'On the Jewish Question'. In his controversial antisemitic pamphlet *The Jewish Question* (1843), Bauer had written: 'Just as the gods of Epicurus live in the interstices of the world, where they are relieved of specific work, so the Jews have fixed themselves outside specific class and corporate interests.'[18] The antisemitic victim-blaming implicit in Bauer's imagery ('the Jews have fixed themselves') contrasts with the materialist sociology of Marx – and ultimately of Trotsky and Leon – which grounds racism and racial difference in the political economy.

The unfolding of the metaphor through which the social status of the Jews is imagined is as instructive as is the different political valence attached to their social status. While the epicurean cosmology belongs to Bauer, the bodily metaphor of Jews as pores on the surface of the skin begins with Marx. While introducing a mixed metaphor – grafting onto Epicurus the comparison of Jews to the 'pores of Polish society' – Marx portrayed the Jewish people not as symbols of modern capitalism, but rather as 'representatives of the pre-capitalist market economy'.[19] Over the course of his book, Leon works wonders with Marx's dense but obscure comparison of Jews in Polish society to pores on skin. He may have been inspired to develop the pore metaphor by Trotsky, who in 1940 wrote that the 'decaying capitalist society is striving to squeeze the Jewish people from all its pores'.[20]

In the most common usage, a pore is an 'opening in the skin or body surface of an animal'; biologically it marks 'the opening of the duct of a sweat gland or sebaceous gland'.[21] The word derives from Greek via Latin, Middle English, and Old French. The Greek *poros* refers to a passage or opening. The comparison of Jews to pores captivated Leon's imagination. Since Marx had given it a specifically Polish twist, Leon's fascination was understandable in light of his Polish background. And yet Leon developed Marx's metaphor even further, making it the foundation of his undeclared critique of the early Marx's account of the relation between Jews and capitalism. In Leon's expanded version of Marx's metaphor, the dissolution of feudalism involved the expulsion of the 'elements which were, at one and the same time, foreign to it and indispensable to it'. Pores cover the skin's surface, enabling essential gases, liquids, and particles to pass into the body. They are both extrinsic to the body and necessary for its survival. This parallels the role of Jews within feudal society – a role that persisted in modified form under capitalism. The metaphor of Jew-as-pore enabled Leon both to challenge the implicit antisemitism of socialists like Sombart and to ground his critique of capitalism in its constriction of Jews' economic horizons.

While the Marx of *Capital* more closely prefigures Leon's book, Leon goes further even than the late Marx in outlining the role of the political economy in the development of the Jews as a people, and in their subsequent ostracization. Likewise, he goes further than Trotsky in grounding his scattered reflections on antisemitism in a deeply grounded account of Jewish history. Although Leon wrote under the most difficult conditions imaginable, he managed to assemble an impressive if eclectic array of sources, ranging from French, German, and English historians, including Fustel de Coulanges and Henri Pirenne, to obscure Yiddish studies of the mountaineers of Daghestan.

Given that it was the Israeli conflict that stimulated interest in his work during the 1960s, it is ironic that Leon says little in his book about Israel or Zionism as such. Instead, he develops a materialist critique of the social and economic role of the Jews throughout history, from the Roman conquest to the Renaissance. In keeping with his Marxist and Trotskyist framework, class and socioeconomic status are the primary movers in his analysis. 'Only a study of the economic role played by the Jews', he wrote, 'can contribute to elucidating the causes for "the miracle of the Jew"' – by which he means the Jewish people's survival amid millennia of persecution.[22] Leon channelled and internalized Marx's insight that 'Judaism has preserved itself not despite history, but by means of history'.[23] Indeed, he took Marx's insight one step further. 'It is not the loyalty of the Jews to their faith which explains their preservation as a distinct social group', Leon wrote; 'on the contrary, it is their preservation as a distinct social group which explains their attachment to their faith.'[24] By contrast, Christians and Muslims had been united through their beliefs even more than through their membership in a social group.

While Leon acknowledged the role of Christianity in creating modern antisemitism, he pointed out that systematic hatred of Jews was older than Christianity itself. The Roman statesman Seneca regarded Jews as 'a criminal race'. The satirical playwright Juvenal 'believed that Jews existed only to cause evil for other people'. For the Roman rhetorician Quintilian, 'the Jews were a curse for other people'.[25] For ancient Romans as for medieval Christians, antisemitism originates in 'class ideology', and in the disdain of the ruling class towards 'all forms of economic activity other than those deriving from agriculture'.[26]

Leon quotes Aristotle to provocative effect: 'money was intended to be used in exchange, but not to increase at interest'.[27] In short, antisemitism arose in the ancient world out of the contempt of the ruling class for the changes money had introduced into the social structure. Aristotle called usury, which was integral to money's new social function as a medium of exchange, 'the birth of money from money', and considered it 'the most unnatural' use for money. While earning interest from cash may have violated the natural order from Aristotle's point of view, it was to become central to the emergent mercantile social order. This concept of money as a form of exchange was fundamental to the Jewish way of life, as it was for other emergent merchant classes. As anarchist David Graeber has argued in his magisterial study of debt, from the earliest periods of recorded history, compound interest has functioned as the glue that binds people together.[28] Much like pores on the surface of society's skin, Jews had to be expelled from time to time, but could never wholly be dispensed with.

While recognizing that antisemitism pre-dated Christianity, Leon concentrated on the impact of the medieval political economy in determining the social and economic role of the Jews. Pithily summarizing the role of Jews within the medieval European political economy, Leon stated: 'The Jews despoiled the lords and the kings fleeced the Jews.'[29] Jewish moneylenders were useful to the king because they kept in check the power of the nobility and enabled the king to exert power indirectly over the lords of the land. In an era before cash was the ultimate source of economic value, the king was able to use the financial capital of the Jews to entrench his sovereign power across his dominion. He consolidated his economic reserves by imposing high taxes on the profits made by Jews during the course of their moneylending activities. The result was a political equilibrium that granted a measure of peace and security to the Jews, yet which would be undone by capitalism.

Once workers were able to generate their own surplus value – to buy and sell whatever they needed on the market without the mediation of a moneylender – Jews came to be seen as what sociologist Max Weber would call a 'pariah people'.[30] While Weber's interpretation of Judaism has been criticized for assuming that the Jews consented to their marginalization and economic disenfranchisement, his account contains the seeds of later critiques of antisemitism. As Italian-Jewish historian Arnaldo Momigliano notes, Weber's 'sympathetic understanding of the rabbis, against the entire tradition of German scholarship, is perhaps the most remarkable feature of Weber's interpretation of Judaism'.[31] Like Marx and Trotsky, Leon took from Weber the insights that best served his historical-materialist critique, while dispensing with those aspects of Weber's interpretation that denied Jewish agency.

Leon acknowledges many parallels between the economic activity of the Jewish merchant class and the gradual rise of capitalism. Yet he also emphasizes the differences between the economic impact of the European bourgeoisie on the development of capitalism and traditional Jewish mercantilism, which did not generate surplus value. For Leon, the key difference between the bourgeoisie and the Jews is that Jews did not introduce a new mode of production into the sociopolitical order. Instead, they adapted their economic activities to existing social structures, just as they had done in prior eras. Contrary to the widespread view that Jewish mercantile activity ushered in capitalist accumulation, or that Jews directly profited from capitalism, Leon insists that capitalism *assimilated* Jews and incorporated them into its socioeconomic structure, with the inevitable consequence of their disappearance. According to this view, Judaism flourished more in Eastern Europe than in western Europe precisely because Eastern Europe was further removed from capitalist modes of production. 'In its convulsions', Leon writes, 'capitalism cast out even those Jewish elements which it has not yet completely assimilated.'[32] In line with the impoverishment of the Jews as a social class that accompanied the rise of capitalism, '"Jewish banks" were no longer anything but pawnshops where it is poverty which is the borrower.'[33]

Throughout the book, Leon's focus is on the role of capitalism in enabling the marginalization of the Jews. 'Capitalism has posed the Jewish problem, that is to say, has destroyed the social basis upon which Judaism maintained itself for centuries', he writes. 'But capitalism has not resolved the Jewish problem, for it has been unable to absorb the Jew liberated from his social shell.'[34] With Marx, Leon recognizes the benefits of modern industrialization, but also the fact that those benefits could not be experienced by Jews due to their prior marginalization. Whereas before capitalism Jews were located within the pores of mainstream society, now they are frozen, in limbo: 'the decline of capitalism has suspended the Jews between heaven and earth'. The Jewish mercantile class had largely disappeared by the time of Leon's writing, yet the next generation 'has found no place in modern production'. Leon draws a dramatic conclusion from this social-economic evolution: 'There is no solution to the Jewish problem under capitalism, just as there is no solution to the other problems posed before humanity, without profound social upheavals.'[35]

The two concluding chapters of Leon's book, devoted to antisemitism after World War I, are particularly relevant to our political moment for the light they shed on debates around antisemitism after the widespread adoption of the IHRA defintion. In these chapters, Leon applies his historical–sociological mode of analysis to his contemporary environment. This leads to a penetrating diagnosis of the fate of capitalism in a post-Marxian age. In his own words, Jews are the first 'to be eliminated by decaying feudalism', and also 'the first to be rejected by the convulsions of dying capitalism'. They are 'wedged between the anvil of decaying feudalism and the hammer of rotting capitalism'.[36] Developing the Marxist insight that ideology is a form of false consciousness that masks the material factors that truly motivate action, Leon aligns his materialist critique of antisemitism with the critique of other forms of racism.

He begins by noting how Hitler created a homogenous enemy from a multitude of non-Germanic peoples in order to mobilize hatred against it. Without this illusion of homogeneity, demagogues like Hitler understood that 'the masses will start thinking too much about the differences which exist among those enemies'. Their hatred would dissipate, making political action against so-called enemies more difficult. In short, Leon understands racism as a myth that 'demands faith' and which 'fears reason like the plague'. Leon's analysis of racism is consistent with the internationalism of Trotsky and other Marxists, but develops these ideas in a more historically grounded way. Given his insight that forced homogeneity fosters racism, Leon's opposition to Zionism, a movement that seeks to homogenize Jews into a single nation, makes sense.

Among the most perceptive observations Leon makes is that, of all the many forms of race hatred, 'antisemitism contributes the most to cementing the different elements of racism'.[37] In Nazi Germany, antisemitism was the glue that united various non-Germanic peoples and social outcasts, including the Roma and homosexuals, into a common enemy. Antisemitism functioned in this way after the Holocaust as well, as Frantz Fanon recognized when he quoted his teacher from the Antilles: 'When you hear someone insulting the Jews pay attention; he is talking about you.' Only later did Fanon understand that his teacher's point was specifically connected to the nature of antisemitism, which incorporates many different kinds of racism. Alternatively, we could say that racism based on skin colour incorporates the specific strand of antisemitism. As Fanon noted, his teacher simply meant that 'the anti-Semite is inevitably a negrophobe'.[38] Fanon wrote these words in 1952, a decade after Leon had touched on the same intersection of racism and antisemitism from occupied Belgium.

Like Fanon, Leon understood capitalism in the context of imperialism. Rather than treating antisemitism as a phenomenon distinct unto itself, his discussion of antisemitism in the concluding chapters to his book is entirely enfolded within a discussion of racism. 'Racism', Leon writes, is first and foremost 'the ideological disguise of modern imperialism' that is internal to the capitalist world order.[39] Elsewhere, Leon alludes to the role of British imperialism in helping Zionist settlers gain a foothold in Palestine and fight the Arab resistance.[40] The 'support' of British imperialism is harmful to Jews in the long run, Leon insists, indirectly challenging Montagu's insights, but in a more politically attenuated context. He refers specifically to Hitler's concept of *Lebensraum* (the race struggling for its 'living space', which was used to justify the Third Reich's territorial expansion into Eastern Europe) as an example of 'the permanent necessity for expansion which characterizes finance or monopoly capitalism'.[41] The 'monopoly capitalism' of big business is contrasted to the 'speculative-commercial capital' that had accounted for the bulk of Jewish economic activity for millennia, until it was subsumed by capitalism during the Industrial Revolution.

From Lenin to Trotsky, many early-twentieth-century leftist commentators on the Jewish question tended to reduce Judaism to a religious creed. On that basis, they have underestimated the need for the collective liberation of the Jewish people specifically as Jews. Leon takes a different approach, which is at once more nuanced and more consistent with the experience of Jewish history. He recognizes Judaism as a religion while insisting on its secular dimensions before modernity, which in his view were destroyed by capitalism. Contrary to the dominant model, Judaism according to Leon was not secularized by modernity. Rather, Judaism was deprived of its intrinsic secularity by modern capitalism, and by its dependence on mercantile exchange.[42] While Jews before modernity dominated the popular imagination as moneylenders, Leon offers a much more variegated account of Jews' social roles before modernity, precisely because he looks beyond European history.

Alongside his intersectional framing of antisemitism, Leon offers a wide-ranging critique of Zionism that is all the more persuasive in light of his prominent role within the Zionist movement prior to his departure from it. Leon frames his critique of Zionism by contrasting his materialist critique of antisemitism with the Zionist approach to this same problem. Leon's materialism compels him 'to make a complete and continuous circuit: from reality to theoretical scheme and the reverse'.[43] This movement between the economic base and the ideological superstructure makes Leon's critique of antisemitism dialectical. This dialectical dimension sets it apart from the nominalist obsessions with definitions that are dominant today, and that underwrite the political deployment of the IHRA definition. Unlike Leon's dialectical materialism, Zionism has no use for history. Leon argues that Zionism 'saves itself the trouble of studying various forms of antisemitism and their evolution'. Instead of such study, Zionist ideology 'transposes modern antisemitism to all of history', offering a monocausal explanation which leads to an oversimplified solution that is too abstract to represent an effective challenge to everyday racism.

Although an account of the fate of the Jewish people undertaken while a genocide was underway might be expected to be a darkly pessimistic book, in fact Leon ends his work with hope. While recognizing that 'the fate of the Jews has never been so tragic', he also insists that 'it has never been so close to ceasing to be that'. In other words, the antisemitism of previous eras, which was rooted in socioeconomic factors, has, by the time he was writing, lost all contact with the material conditions that fostered it. Whereas Jews as a social class had historically been unable to make common cause with other oppressed peoples, in the new revolutionary era that framed Leon's horizons and inspired his activism, 'the interests of the Jewish classes are closely bound up with the interests of the popular masses of the entire world'.[44]

A Materialist Afterlife

When Leon was murdered in Auschwitz at the age of twenty-six, the life of his magnum opus had only just begun. A pivotal moment in the book's trajectory took place during a meeting between the Lebanese intellectual Imad Nuwayhid and his teacher, French Jewish Marxist scholar and professor Maxim Rodinson, at a Paris cafe in 1968. Nuwayhid had travelled to France in search of education and professional training. Although he mostly dedicated his residence in Europe to training in his chosen career of hospitality management, Nuwayhid also took the time to study with Rodinson, who was then France's preeminent Marxist Orientalist. During one of their sessions, Rodinson advised Nuwayhid to take up a new translation project: Leon's book on the Jewish question.

At the time when Rodinson recommended it for translation, Leon's book had been forgotten. In addition to facilitating its translation into Arabic, Rodinson was heavily involved in giving the original French version of Leon's book a second life. He was the main editor of the second edition of the book, which was released in 1968. As Rodinson explained in the essay that accompanied that edition, he had corrected many typographical errors and bibliographic mistakes from the previous edition. He also authored the most important critique of Leon's thesis concerning Jews as a 'people-class' to date; but that did not stop him from also being one of the book's most important champions.[45] Since it was the second edition from which translations were made into other languages, Leon's work benefited greatly from Rodinson's editorial labour. It was in the midst of these editorial activities that Rodinson suggested to Nuwayhid that he translate Leon's book from French into Arabic.

Nuwayhid followed his teacher's advice. Working frantically, within thirty days he had produced the first ever Arabic translation of Leon's book. This was one of the few translations to render the French title accurately, as *The Materialist Concept of the Jewish Question* (*Al-mafhum al-maddi li-l-masalat al-yahudiyyah*), thereby – however inadvertently – recalling the Epicurean materialism that Marx developed into a dialectical-materialist movement towards political liberation. The translation was published the following year in Beirut.[46] Six years later, Nuwayhid would himself be dead, at the young age of thirty-one.[47] During the eventful final years of his life, he joined the Lebanese Communist Party, received military training to defend Palestinians, and was assassinated during the Lebanese Civil War. At the time of his death, Nuwayhid had been fighting for the Lebanese National Movement, which was fighting Israel alongside the Palestinian Liberation Organization. By 1969, in the aftermath of the Six-Day War, Nuwayhid's translation had become a foundational text among leftists for the critique of Israel and the refutation of Zionism. It is easy to understand the appeal of Leon's account of Jewish history and his critique of Zionism for an Arab audience, even though the majority of the book is less concerned with Zionism than with the relationship between antisemitism and capitalism.

Although Leon's book went through many further editions during the 1960s and 1970s, it has by and large been relegated to a footnote within mainstream Jewish studies. When I asked a well-known scholar of antisemitism about the reasons for this neglect, he responded as follows: 'Although the scope of the book is impressive its utility today is hobbled by Leon's economic reductionism: both with regard to antisemitism and the persistence of Jews as a social group.' He then suggested that Leon's materialist approach explained why the book is 'more read within Trotskyite groups than among academic historians'. This criticism is valid, as is the analysis of its consequences; yet I hope I have shown how much Leon's materialist critique offers our polarized environment, in which nominalist definition-based logics have suppressed materially grounded and intersectional accounts of anti-Jewish racism.

Our contemporary understanding of antisemitism has been impoverished by the suppression of materialist approaches like Leon's, and this accounts in part for the peculiar power that definitions have had in recent years to frame our understanding of antisemitism. Simplistic definitions like the one promoted by the IHRA replace the materiality of antisemitism – including its role in racialization and discrimination – with abstract polemics relating to attitudes to Israel. A materialist approach to antisemitism, by contrast, focuses on the lived experience of discrimination and marginalization, while de-emphasizing alignment with a political position. Since politics itself is historically contingent, the experience of exploitation matters more to a materialist agenda than any abstract position. By the time that the IHRA definition was introduced, the Marxian tradition of Jewish historiography that had flourished from the beginning of the twentieth century until the 1970s had almost entirely vanished. When a Hebrew translation of Leon's foundational work was finally published for the first time in 2016, a commentator correctly remarked that the 'Marxist stream' had simply been eradicated from Jewish historiography.[48] While that eradication is partly a result of the decimation of the revolutionary socialist Jewish communities of Eastern Europe during the Holocaust, the process was accelerated by the State of Israel's promotion of Zionism over other ideologies rooted in Jewish history. From the 1920s to the 1940s, the most radical currents of Marxism itself – notably, those affiliated with Trotsky – were often inflected with a Jewish orientation. By this, I mean an attentiveness to the reality of the persecution of the Jews throughout history and a commitment to forging a path towards collective and universal liberation grounded in the experience of antisemitism. Leon's book on the Jewish question is an embodiment of that ethos. That world is now gone. It has been replaced by a toxic and dangerous hostility between Zionists who claim to represent the only Jewish perspective on antisemitism and leftists who are intrinsically hostile to everything linked to Zionism. While there are good reasons for opposing Zionism, as Greek economist and politician Yanis Varoufakis once wisely said while warning against the tendency of anti-capitalism to merge with antisemitism, 'Hatred is not a good guide. Criticism is what we need, and criticism requires depth and not epidermic simple interpretations.'[49] Indeed, far too much of the debate around Zionism today suffers from oversimplification and superficiality. The widespread influence of the IHRA definition and of related efforts to crack down on speech critical of Israel results directly from this stagnation.

Meanwhile, the eradication of the Marxian critique of antisemitism has obscured from view one of the most important resources in fighting antisemitism: dialectical materialism. Leon lucidly reveals the dialectical dimension of his argument when he explains that the emergent science of sociology – then being formulated by Weber, Tönnies, and Simmel – calls for a new orientation: 'from reality to theoretical scheme and the reverse.'[50] As for the materialism that he sees as embodied in Marx's claim that 'Judaism has preserved itself not despite history, but by means of history', Leon insists on it from the opening pages of his book.

Indeed, Leon's complaint that Jewish history 'is one of the few fields of history where idealist prejudices have succeeded in entrenching and maintaining themselves' resonates to this day, particularly in the aftermath of the adoption of the IHRA definition.[51]

Among the idealist prejudices criticized by Leon is messianic Zionism, which he rejects because it postulates an unalienable Jewish right to a specific territory. Against such idealism, Leon insists that 'only a study of the economic role played by the Jews can contribute to elucidating the causes for the "miracle of the Jew"'.[52] Leon's insistence that economic analysis can account for the persistence of Jews throughout history may seem excessively dogmatic – but it is a useful counterweight to the abstract nominalism which dominates the study of antisemitism to this day, and which has contributed to the entrenchment of the IHRA definition. The idealistic approach to Jewish history that Leon criticizes has articulated contingent definitions as transhistorical dogma, rendering them impervious to change. What if, instead of trying to define antisemitism once and for all, we took seriously the dialectical materialism of Jewish Marxists like Leon, Deutscher, and Trotsky, and developed an approach to anti-Jewish racism that is rooted in socioeconomic history? Like other kinds of xenophobia and racism, antisemitism is best understood as a conflagration of illusions and hatred ignited by a failure to grasp one's socioeconomic condition accurately. Materialism furnishes the means to interrogate – and obliterate – such racism more effectively than any definition can achieve.

Why Materialism Now?

What do these reflections on the historical trajectory of the Jewish Question mean for the fight against antisemitism in the twenty-first century, an era dominated by abstract definitions that conceive of antisemitism as a problem that is manifested in belief, speech, and words rather than material conditions and entrenched hierarchies? There are three specific advantages that the materialist approach has over the nominalism of a priori definitions of racism. First, historical materialism provides a foundation for a genuinely intersectional approach to racism. Leon's account of capitalist exploitation, as expressed in his insight that 'racism is in the first place the ideological disguise of modern imperialism', shares much in common with the work of later theorists of racial capitalism that focused on histories of slavery in the African diaspora.[53] He was able to foresee many of the insights that would later be articulated by key theorists of racial capitalism, such as Cedric Robinson and C. L. R. James, because his materialist approach to ideas – including antisemitic ideas – showed him that they should not be taken at face value. Materialism avoids the exceptionalism inculcated by Zionism, instead attending to the social and economic conditions that generate xenophobic prejudice, and which are experienced by many groups in different times and places. Whereas definitions like that of the IHRA do not allow for thinking of antisemitism as a kind of racism, the materialist sees antisemitism within the wider framework of racism, recognizing that both originate in economic inequality. Of course, this does not mean that ideas are ever entirely irrelevant; but a materialist approach recognizes that the views that we consciously hold may not tell the full story, and must be assessed alongside their material context.

Secondly, in contrast to the nominalism of definition-based approaches to racism, the materialist approach is attentive to historical change and contingency. It is less interested in defining a concept once and for all than in attending to how it is modified and reconfigured over time, as political and economic conditions change. The materialist understands that racism is bound up with changing historical norms, and cannot be grasped apart from those norms. A corollary of this is that, if racism is the product of historical and socioeconomic conditions, to the extent that these conditions can be changed, racism can eventually be abolished.

Finally, and perhaps most distinctively in the context of the contemporary debate around antisemitism, a materialist approach never loses sight of the wider framework within which the struggle against antisemitism takes place. It does not consider antisemitism in isolation from other factors, particularly free speech and economic exploitation. When an academic or writer finds their livelihood threatened due to accusations of antisemitism, a materialist will situate the accusations in a wider conceptual framework, taking account of the dangers of allowing even legitimate criticisms of antisemitism to undermine civil liberties, due process, and freedom of expression. This is in specific and direct contrast not just to nominalist definitions of antisemitism, but even to more progressive approaches such as the reservoir theory of antisemitism, which I discuss in Chapter 4. Whereas other approaches to antisemitism that reject the IHRA definition also emphasize intersectionality and historical contingency, the materialist approach is unique in enabling us to view antisemitism within the broader framework of the political economy, and thereby suggests how the struggle against antisemitism might also advance the struggle for collective liberation. Due to its broad sociological view of antisemitism, a materialist foundation for anti-racist mobilization is best suited to protecting freedom of speech.

Trotsky, Leon, and Deutscher understood antisemitism dialectically, as a means of keeping in place an established social order that normalized Jewish suffering. They understood antisemitism as the product of socioeconomic conditions rather than as a clash of beliefs or religious ideologies, or as a set of words and tropes that ought to be banned. They understood that the socioeconomic medium through which social and cultural differences are experienced can never be neutral. Their approach has significant implications for how we ought to think about antisemitism in the twenty-first century, after the widespread adoption of the IHRA definition.

In order to demonstrate the potential of a materialist critique of antisemitism in an era dominated by nominal definitions, we must first distinguish between the idealist approach criticised by Leon, which holds that things cannot exist until they are named, and materialism, which holds that being determines and precedes consciousness. The latter position is well captured in Marx's famous dictum: 'Being determines consciousness' (*Das Sein bestimmt das Bewusstsein*). Stated otherwise, this means that the conditions into which we are born shape the most basic aspects of how we think about others. Our material conditions determine how we experience racism. Leon demonstrates throughout his work that the prevalence of antisemitism in successive historical epochs is correlated to the socioeconomic status of Jews within that era. This does not mean antisemitism is justified, but simply that the conditions that give rise to it have an empirical basis, and our critique should therefore by directed at that empirical foundation.

The idealist approach to antisemitism exemplified by the IHRA definition occupies the opposite pole of this spectrum. Whereas the materialist recognizes that racism originates in social conditions, the idealist seeks to resolve antisemitism by defining it. But defining is not understanding: every definition recreates the object being defined in its own image. In philosophy, this is called reification. The formulaic insistence that in order to oppose antisemitism we must first define it is one of the most recurrent slogans used by those who promote the adoption of the IHRA definition.[54] Idealism unhelpfully inverts the materialist approach advocated by Leon. A definitional approach to racism assumes that the act of naming determines the reality to which the name refers, rather than the other way around. Hence, in naming antisemitism, proponents of the IHRA definition exert control over the narrative around it. The power to name antisemitism morphs into control over Jewish identity itself, and other issues tangentially related to this conflict – Israel; Palestine; the scope, range, and legitimacy of leftist activism – are swept up into this monolithic narrative.

The problem with the idealist approach to antisemitism is that it leads to political stagnation and simplifies the challenge of combating racism. In addition, it silences those who do not agree or consent to the idealist position. When the fight against anti-semitism becomes restricted to the act of naming it, we are bound to lose sight of the conditions that create it. But it is the conditions that generate racism rather than the words associated with it that must be overturned in order to bring antisemitism to an end. When words are elevated over material conditions, the fight against antisemitism is reduced to a battle for control over the right to name. Any effort to overturn the conditions of anti-semitism's genesis is thereby undermined. The illusion of action that nominalist and idealist definitions facilitate obscures the ways in which antisemitism continues to flourish in places where proponents of the IHRA definition are least likely to look: government policies that are favourable to Israel and laws that ban criticism of Israel.

The great advantage that the materialist critique of anti-semitism has over the idealist approach is that it is politically actionable. Materialism supports free speech by virtue of the wide lens through which it views antisemitism, and through its rejection of an isolated approach to individual instances of antisemitism. Its intersectionality also strengths the free-speech position by creating solidarity across divisions of time, space, and history. Following Marx, materialism aims not merely to rename the world for political ends, but to *change* it. A materialist critique of antisemitism intervenes in the conditions that give rise to racism, rather than merely redefining or reifying a certain pattern of prejudice. Far from being deterministic, materialism recognizes that the economic exploitation that generated antisemitism is contingent in its own way, and is therefore subject to change, and ultimately obliteration. While it realistically recognizes the depth and breadth of antisemitism, it opposes antisemitism dialectically, by resisting the conditions that generate it, rather than through the deployment of definitional abstractions.

Only within a materialistic framework could a Jew such as Leon, soon to be annihilated in the Nazi genocide, find common ground for solidarity between an antisemitic peasant and a Jewish usurer. As he states – somewhat shockingly, given the circumstances in which he was writing – of a hypothetical European peasant who was overcome by hatred of a hypothetical Jewish usurer who was exploiting him: 'It is easy to understand the hatred that the man of the people must have felt for the Jew in whom he saw the direct cause of his ruin'.[55] In the act of making sense of antisemitism within medieval European society, Leon paradoxically dissolves the idealist foundations of racialized hate. The moment when two people whose political interests are pitted against each other are brought into relation by the materialist who observes at a distance, centuries later, is the moment when the power of racializing stereotypes fades away, and class-based solidarity – rooted in material conditions – triumphs. Of course, this solidarity is forged within Leon's materialist imagination, and is not necessarily present in the medieval historical record. Yet it remains an historical fact that, in Nazi-occupied Belgium, a courageous Jewish intellectual fought antisemitism through a materialist critique of economic inequality. His critique – his courage, integrity, and refusal to derive consolation from false consciousness or Jewish exceptionalism – remains an inspiration to this day.

Leon's critique of antisemitism holds out hope for the future through its ambitious and radical – if somewhat underdeveloped – materialist historiography. Yet nothing remotely resembling the eradication of antisemitism has happened following the adoption of the IHRA, or of any other definition of antisemitism. Definitions are not the solution to the problem of antisemitism, or to any other racism, and it is simplistic to posit any definition as a progressive act. The adoption of the IHRA definition by government agencies and their proxies merely entails a nominal switch, from one name (EUMC) to another (IHRA). No fundamental reworking of the social order has transpired, or will do so, as a result of such adoptions. Instead of definitions, we need a radical materialist critique of antisemitism that perceives its connection with other racisms, refuses to abstract it from the socioeconomic foundations that make antisemitism possible, and prioritizes (rather than simply 'balances') freedom of expression. Although the alliances between the struggle against antisemitism and radical leftist materialism have not been as strong in recent years as they might have been, Leon's detailed critique shows us that materialism provides a much more effective toolkit for resisting antisemitism and other racisms than does definition-based idealism. The latter leaves its proponents feeling like they have accomplished something while in fact they have only achieved the suppression of free speech.

The idealist approach to combating antisemitism is a legitimate target for David Feldman's critical insight that 'antisemitism is too often seen as a political problem to be faced down rather than an ethical problem to be confronted'.[56] As Feldman and Marc Volovici write elsewhere, 'Definitions present themselves with a spurious objectivity. They hide the different political purposes to which frequently they are tied.'[57] No doubt the low-maintenance approach to fighting antisemitism that the definitional fixation involves explains its appeal for the politicians and other public figures who threaten those who resist its adoption with punishment while ignoring the consequences of their suppression of the right to protest.

I recognize that this position might in turn seem idealistic, given that we are no longer operating in a world of revolutionary hope or expectation. The communist dream has a very different status in 2022 than it did in 1942, let alone 1917. But you do not have to be a communist – or wish for a communist revolution – in order to perceive the value and utility of the materialist critique of antisemitism today. All that is necessary is that you recognize the many deceptions and sleights of hand, the outright violations of free speech, and the countless undocumented instances of self-censorship that the definitional approach to antisemitism has underwritten during the past several years. If you recognize that the definitional approach is wrong, you will likely also long for a perspective that views Jewish history from the perspective of the *longue durée*, that resonates as true because it is attentive to historical change, and that can see through the lies we tell ourselves and others about why we believe certain things. This is what Leon offers us today.

4

Free Speech and Palestinian Freedom

On 1 October 2021, the unthinkable happened. The University of Bristol announced that it had terminated the employment of David Miller. Miller was a professor of political sociology who specialized in exposing the networks of influence exerted on British and global politics by right-wing pressure groups. This was the first time a faculty member had ever been sacked in a British University specifically as a result of his public criticisms of Israel. The contentious process that led to the termination of Miller's position is of interest to this inquiry into the future of free speech and the critique of antisemitism because of the deep divisions it created within the scholarly world, and the hypocrisies it exposed.

The firing of David Miller was unusual in that the statements that led to Miller's termination were made outside a university venue and during a non-work-related online meeting. Another unprecedented detail of Miller's case is that the university terminated his employment even before he had exercised his right to appeal the decision. The university was either already certain of what the outcome of the appeal would be, or was pressured by external parties to act quickly. Perhaps most paradoxically, the termination occurred after a Queen's Counsel (QC) – a senior trial lawyer – hired by the university had determined that Miller's comments 'did not constitute unlawful speech'.[1] Since Miller was fired by the very same university that had deliberated over calls to fire me in 2017, it is worth asking what specifically it is about the University of Bristol, with its overwhelmingly white and upper-class demographic, that attracts this kind of censorship.

Miller moved to the University of Bristol from a professorial position at the University of Bath in 2018, a year after my departure. I knew of his work, and recall being surprised that the university had been willing to hire such a controversial thinker, who was well known for his criticisms of Israel. All I had witnessed and experienced first-hand regarding the university's unwillingness to engage with Palestinian and other non-Eurocentric points of view led me to expect that Miller would have been greeted with a hostile reception. But when Miller's appointment as professor was approved by the board, university administrators found nothing problematic in his statements or views. This only began to change once external groups began to complain. A similar pattern of administrative response can be detected in the case of Steven Salaita (see below), and indeed my own.

It did not take long after his move to Bristol before controversy began to surround Miller, particularly in connection with his lectures on the role of Zionism in British politics. In these lectures, Miller purported to identify a key networks of Zionist influence within the UK. Many of the organizations Miller named in his lectures – such as the Board of Deputies of British Jews, the Community Security Trust, the Britain Israel Communications and Research Centre (BICOM), and the Jewish Leadership Council – were outraged at being identified as agents of the Israeli state. Allegations of antisemitism soon followed. In 2019, the Community Security Trust lodged a complaint with the University of Bristol, which the university dismissed that same year. In its initial response to external pressure, the university appropriately kept its distance from the controversy, refusing to undertake disciplinary action. Meanwhile, the momentum against Miller grew. A student group, the Jewish Students Society (JSoc), took the lead in blacklisting Miller.

By 2021, as controversies multiplied and indignation spread, Miller persisted in asserting the dangers of Zionism. Two events in February of that year sealed the case against him. The first was an online meeting organized by the campaign group Labour Against the Witchhunt. When the conversation turned to the attacks Miller was facing at Bristol, he made a number of controversial comments. Among these were the claim that the 'Zionist movement' was 'engaged in deliberately fostering Islamophobia', and that Zionism encourages 'Islamophobia and anti-Arab racism too'.[2] Miller also stated during the meeting that the head of JSoc, along with the president of the Union of Jewish Students, had made an official complaint about him to the university – a fact that the complainants themselves had already made public. Miller's reference to this complaint during a non-work-related meeting would provide the foundation for later claims that he had engaged in 'harassment' of Jewish students. Specifically, university authorities informed Miller that his description of the complaint against him as an 'attack' was an act of harassment and grounds for his termination.[3] But, as Miller pointed out, far from targeting individuals, he was merely repeating information that had been placed in the public domain by the complainants themselves.

The second incident followed from the first. Reporters from the *Bristol Tab* and the *Jewish Chronicle* wrote to Miller after the online meeting, asking for his comments on the controversy they had caused. Miller doubled down on his previous statements, writing to the *Bristol Tab*: 'This is on the record: Zionism is and always has been a racist, violent, imperialist ideology premised on ethnic cleansing. It is an endemically anti-Arab and Islamophobic ideology. It has no place in any society.'[4]

Although these statements were certainly within the bounds of free speech, they were problematic for other reasons. Miller's dogmatic insistence that Zionism 'has no place in any society' ironically mirrored in its absolutism the rhetoric of those who advocated firing him. Both sides reverted to an a priori – and notably non-materialist – ideal of how the world ought to be, insisting on either side that there was 'no place' for Zionism or for racism, rather than how it actually was. Neither side was willing to listen to the other. Declaring that racism 'has no place in any society' is a turn of phrase commonly resorted to by politicians keen to brandish the purity of their politics. This technique operates at the opposite end of the political spectrum, as for example in Conservative prime minster Theresa May's declaration in 2018 that 'antisemitism and misogyny have no place in this country'.[5] Performative dismissals like these often function as substitutes for meaningful engagement. By declaring that a given ideology 'has no place in any society' the speaker showcases their opposition to it. They purify themselves of its taint without achieving anything concrete. Meanwhile, the political need to recognize that the tainted ideology is in fact an *intrinsic* part of our society is perpetually deferred. Blame is shifted onto something else, be it Zionism, racism, or the perpetual spectre of antisemitism. Such blame-shifting rhetoric prevents us from properly interrogating the problems within our societies and within ourselves. We become distracted and preoccupied with the mandate to seek purification from a taint in which we are already implicated.

I was and remain opposed to Miller's termination not because I supported his views. Miller's work on Syria is to my mind even more troubling than his statements about Zionism.[6] His sociological method sometimes reduces humans to the systems in which they are enmeshed, evacuating them of nuance and complexity. In light of this tendency, many have perceived parallels between Miller's approach to politics and the conspiratorial thinking that undergirds antisemitism in its most recognizable forms. For example, Miller consistently refers to Israel as a hostile foreign power, without registering the more nuanced aspects of Israel's influence on European and American public discourse, which is very much one of fraternity and connection rather than hostility. This does not make Israel's influence any less harmful, just more rooted in actual geopolitics. Even more problematically, all foreign influence is treated within Miller's system as though it were inherently evil, without recognizing how much the world has benefited from international exchange, including government-sponsored initiatives.

While Israel has had a negative influence on Euro-American public debate, it does not follow that foreign influence as such is malevolent. Indeed, it is disorientating to a hear a committed anti-racist such as Miller implicitly endorse a nationalist ideology that treats Israel as the archenemy – as a 'hostile foreign entity', as if the integrity of the British state was worth defending – without mentioning British complicity in settler-colonial projects. For example, in his critical commentary on Miller's dismissal, political theorist Alex Callinicos points out that the geopolitical alignment between western states and Israel 'isn't a product of the lobby's influence, but a convergence of interests'.[7] To blame Israel exclusively for the suppression of dissent against Israel and pro-Palestinian activism in European and North American democracies is in fact to understate the extent of the problem, which is rooted in the erosion of civil liberties broadly rather than in the influence of a single lobby group. Miller is also critical of British imperialism, but he nonetheless chooses to fixate on Israel. Leaving aside the accusation of antisemitism, this approach is analytically problematic because it blinds us to our own, more proximate complicity.

Whatever Miller's views, however, he has an absolute right to speak the truth as he sees it, no matter how misguided, simplified, or even offensive his perceptions are to some. That nothing Miller said or did amounted to a fireable offense was confirmed by a report from the QC hired by the university to investigate the charges against him. While the university chose not to make this report public, an earlier report, which the university had commissioned following the complaints of 2019, was leaked to the media soon after Miller's termination.[8] In this report, the lawyer concluded: 'there is no case to answer against Professor Miller in connection with any of the matters I have investigated', thereby sealing the contradiction between private exoneration and public punishment.

94

After the report was leaked, two lecturers at the university circulated five questions addressed to the administration.[9] They wanted to know how academic freedom would be upheld by the university after such a monumental decision. Pertinently, they asked whether the administration's decisions and policies could be 'guaranteed to remain independent of political lobbying', given the ample evidence that it had caved in to pressure from MPs in its decision to fire Miller. Finally, given that Miller's most controversial statements occurred outside any university context or workplace environment, they wanted to know, 'When are we, as academics, representing the University, and when are we not?' At the time of writing, every one of these urgent questions remains unanswered by the university.

Although Miller was a longstanding member of the University and College Union (UCU), the UCU itself failed to support him publicly at the national level. When my article was under fire, I similarly witnessed the UCU's hesitation to take academic freedom seriously. Although the UCU did provide casework support, which consisted of advice and guidance by branch members, I only genuinely began to feel supported when I hired a lawyer from the law firm Bindmans to support me directly. Miller's local branch, the Bristol UCU, did issue a motion in March 2021, when the investigation was just beginning, and called it 'a test case for the interpretation of Statutes that affects everyone at the University'.[10] But the union was conspicuously silent after he was dismissed. He did receive legal representation through UCU, but, as a Bristol branch UCU member and departmental colleague of Miller commented, UCU 'seem strangely reluctant to link to [a] wider campaign for academic freedom . . . [The branch] resolved in early summer to ensure that UoB followed "due process" in the investigation, but the union has not taken a position on subsequent dismissal. So far [Bristol] UCU have not responded to our [departmental] rep's questions.'[11] As noted by this colleague, no statement was issued and no protest followed from the branch. Britain's professional association of scholars of the Middle East, the British Society for Middle Eastern Studies, did write to the university on multiple occasions. Each time its letters were ignored.

The controversy around the termination of Miller's employment proved what many have always known: so much of the discussion that claims to be about free speech is actually about something else. Cambridge student Talal Hangari, who had recently been removed from his position within a student Labour club for his criticism of the IHRA definition, has condemned 'the tendency of the contemporary left to refrain from defending anyone's right to speak unless it can defend their each and every utterance. Where this is difficult, you often find silence. Hence Miller has not seen support for his free speech rights across much of the left.'[12] This is exactly true in the case Miller. Many of his ideas cannot reasonably be defended. Some are simply wrong. In this respect, however, he resembles most provocative thinkers. From the vantage point of free speech, there is nothing wrong with being wrong. What is wrong – in the sense that it distracts us from political freedom – is the prevalent notion that we should only defend those with whom we agree in all respects. The basis for our solidarity with Miller need not be agreement, and it my view it is better that it not be. Miller should be defended, along with every other activist who has faced bad-faith accusations, because the liberty that we defend when we insist on Miller's right to speak the truth as he sees it is the same liberty that Palestinians themselves deserve and rightly demand under the conditions of occupation.

In order to grasp fully what happened to Miller – and to understand why the university community looked the other way while his academic freedom was violated – we need to situate it alongside the cases of other violations of academic freedom. As it happens, at the time of Miller's firing there were at least two other campaigns underway at UK universities to get academics fired. One was against Steven Greer, another professor at the University of Bristol. Another targeted Kathleen Stock, a philosopher and gender-critical feminist at the University of Sussex. Comparing these three cases reveals a double – or triple – standard when it comes to complaints of antisemitism in the contemporary political environment, particularly when these complaints are tied to criticisms of Israel. Further, across each of these cases, the comparison exposes a systematic neglect of both the grievances that motivate complaints *and* the free speech issues that they raise. Far from being in tension with each other, the same universities that violate their employees' and students' free-speech rights also fail to take seriously their complaints of harassment and discrimination.

Simultaneously with the university's proceedings against Miller, a parallel investigation was underway at Bristol into a complaint made by the president of the university's Islamic Society (BRISOC) against Greer, a long-time professor of human rights in the University of Bristol Law School. The BRISOC president complained that Greer's module 'Islam, China and the Far East' was riddled with Islamophobia. He also objected to Greer's defence of the controversial UK counter-terrorism legislation known as Prevent, which targets Muslims for state surveillance and encourages teachers, nurses, and social workers to report students deemed at risk to the authorities.[13] The complaint against Greer was lodged on October 2020, between the exoneration of Miller by the university for his controversial teaching and his more controversial statements of February 2021. Out of frustration at the university's inaction, BRISOC made its complaint public while it was still pending, on 20 February 2021 – within a week of Miller's controversial comments about Zionism. The publication of the BRISOC complaint during this period strongly suggests that the students' opposition to Greer was influenced by the proceedings against Miller and the Islamophobic atmosphere they had fostered.

The complaint claimed that the Islamophobic tendencies of Greer's lectures revealed 'an institutional failing to understand how this kind of rhetoric will cause harm; not only to Muslim students in his classes but also in the way these ideas will deepen divisions between Muslims and the wider society'. In a symptom of the censorious atmosphere that has overtaken university campuses, the complaint demanded that 'disciplinary action be taken' against Greer, 'including suspension and/or dismissal'. While such demands are themselves injurious to free speech and academic freedom, the perspectives voiced in this document attest to a widespread sense among Bristol's Muslim students that they were being ignored, even as extra vigilance was applied to statements deemed too critical of Israel or too supportive of Palestinian rights. The university took drastic punitive action in response to the accusations of antisemitism against Miller, yet Muslim students' experiences of disenfranchisement were passed over. The university's wider lack of support for scholarly research related to the Islamic world – which I tried without success to change while I was employed there – reinforced Muslim students' sense of marginalization. Although the campaign to fire or punish Greer was damaging to academic freedom, its wider point concerning the university's implicit institutional Islamophobia was borne out by the university's response.

On 8 October 2021, exactly one week after it had announced the termination of Miller, the university officially dismissed the complaint against Greer and formally concluded its investigation of the charge of Islamophobia that had been made by the BRISOC president. Whereas the university announced it was terminating Miller before he had exercised his right of appeal, Greer's exoneration was announced only after a university panel had invalidated the complaint and there was no chance of further appeal. The different treatment accorded to the targets of the complaints illustrates a broader divergence between the two cases. Also striking was the sympathy that was explicitly extended to Greer by the university but denied to those who complained against him. The motion passed by the Bristol branch of the UCU while the investigation into Miller was ongoing referred to the 'abuse, harassment and targeted intimidation of staff who have demonstrated publicly whether on social media or as signatories of open letters their defence of David Miller, his academic freedom and employment rights'. While the university said nothing about how Miller and his colleagues were affected by his termination, they diligently noted in their statement on Greer's exoneration that he had 'been the target of abuse after BRISOC released details of the complaint on social media'.[14] It was a strange spectacle of duplicity, which seemed targeted to send a message to Muslim students that their views and perspectives did not matter as much as those of the Jewish complainants.

Just as I do not defend Miller's writings, neither do I defend Greer's accusers. Both academics were unfairly targeted. The timing chosen for the complaint against Greer indicates that it was retaliation for the attacks on Miller. Yet this unjust targeting was also an inevitable result of the university's bias. A retaliatory atmosphere festers when grievances cannot be freely aired and free speech is suppressed. By choosing secrecy over transparency, the university created a toxic environment for all students. Instead of turning the controversy around Miller's words into a teaching moment, the university engaged in double standards and caved in to external pressures. Greer should not have been punished for inequalities that long preceded him; but the university is culpable for not heeding the students' complaint about the university's historically entrenched ignorance and hostility with regard to Islamic culture and identity.

Ultimately, the story that needs to be told here is not about the University of Bristol. Many universities would have acted the same way in its place, particularly those without a large contingent of Muslim students. The issue we need to focus on is how universities manage conflict, and bury opportunities for debate that could potentially expand students' horizons in legal formulas and abstractions. Definitions like the IHRA's greatly contribute to the bureaucratization of debate – but there are other forces at work as well, including the government's micromanagerial approach to higher education, and legal threats from external organizations. From a managerial point of view, the University of Bristol no doubt knew what it was doing when it shrouded the Miller controversy in veils of secrecy. But the damage it inflicted on free speech in British universities in doing so is permanent and irrevocable.

Structural divergences between the treatment of antisemitism and Islamophobia are manifested time and again in our universities, as they are in society at large. Academics are regularly punished harshly for statements deemed antisemitic, while statements that are experienced as Islamophobic or racist are treated as protected speech. The number of academics in North American and European universities fired due to charges of antisemitism grows every year, while not a single academic has been fired following an accusation of Islamophobia. Although free speech today is often aligned with right-wing movements, historically it has been the decisive factor in leftist political victories. Even today, leftist struggles are debilitated by a failure to consistently use free speech to their advantage. Professors like Greer, whose views align with the state's existing practices, may find their lectures cancelled – an outcome that is unfortunate and harmful to academic freedom – but more often than not they keep their jobs. Other conservative professors, such as geophysicist Dorian S. Abbot of the University of Chicago and Jordan Peterson of the University of Toronto, may be de-platformed for statements perceived as hostile to women and minorities. Controversies stirred by their work may lead them to reschedule or relocate their talks. Meanwhile, professors who advocate agendas that challenge existing power arrangements face more severe risks. Their livelihoods come under threat, as they are more likely to be permanently removed from their posts. While having a lecture cancelled and losing a job can both be frustrating experiences, we should distinguish between the severity of these outcomes. Some free-speech violations are more heinous than others. Right-wing politicians often build momentum in the culture wars around minor inconveniences to freedom of expression, while ignoring the higher stakes involved in the loss of livelihood that their policies bring about.

This trivialization of free speech is one reason why the issue is often made to appear relevant only to affluent demographics and privileged classes. Nonetheless, it is the disenfranchised and the underrepresented who are most in need of the protections afforded by freedom of speech. Having lost faith in the protections afforded by free speech, certain sections of the left are gradually abandoning this principle. The titles of recent books, such as P. E. Moskowitz's *The Case Against Free Speech: The First Amendment, Fascism, and the Future of Dissent* (2019) and Gavin Titley's *Is Free Speech Racist?* (2020), attest to a growing sense of apathy and cynicism towards freedom of speech within leftist political mobilization. When cancel culture merely leads to a forced rescheduling or the relocation of an event to a different venue, the impact is not as pernicious or dangerous as the loss of livelihood. In order to gauge the real state of free speech in liberal democracies, we must reasonably evaluate the harms of censorship according to their real-world impact on peoples' lives. We also need to keep alive the original meaning of free speech, and its roots in the meaning of freedom as such. For any democratic existence, freedom is the core political value, and a precondition for all other political acts.

Speaking freely as a political citizen means exercising the right to criticize and challenge the state. Marc Lamont Hill and Mitchell Plitnick have shown that speaking out on Palestine carries far greater risks than speaking out on other issues, particularly those that align with existing institutional and governmental practices and policies.[15] The list of writers and academics who have lost their jobs as a result of their advocacy for Palestine grows longer every year. In the United States, this trend famously began with Steven Salaita, who was 'de-hired' by the University of Illinois in 2013 in the midst of an Israeli attack on Gaza.[16] In 2021, during another Israeli attack on Gaza, Emily Wilder was fired by the Associated Press for anti-Israel comments she had made while still a university student. In 2020, an offer made by the University of Toronto to Dr Valentina Azarova to head the university's International Human Rights Program at the Faculty of Law was later retracted. It was subsequently revealed that the retraction was linked to concerns expressed by a university donor, who was also a sitting judge, regarding Azarova's scholarly critiques of Israel's human rights record.[17]

Many more Palestine advocates from a remarkably wide range of backgrounds and affiliations have been subjected to censorship in the short term: philosopher Achille Mbembe, gender theorist Judith Butler, human rights advocate Kenneth Roth, and Palestinian-German journalist Nemi El-Hassan have all come under attack in various ways for their support of Palestine. Indeed, in the current climate it would be highly unusual for an ardent pro-Palestine campaigner *not* to be accused of anti-semitism at some point in the course of their work. The Jerusalem Declaration acknowledges this danger, and specifically states that 'supporting the Palestinian demand for justice' is 'not anti-semitism'. Yet, as we will see, this caveat is inadequate, either to protect against the misuse of allegations of antisemitism to suppress pro-Palestinian activism, or to ensure that due process rights and free-speech prerogatives are not violated in the context of this debate.

Although it is a more recent development, the list of activists and scholars who have come under attack as a result of their support for Palestinian rights in the United Kingdom since 2016 is growing at an exponential rate. In 2016, newly elected president of the National Union of Students Malia Bouattia was targeted for her pro-Palestinian statements by groups campaigning against antisemitism.[18] In 2017, Malaka Mohammad was attacked by a well-known group that ostensibly campaigns against antisemitism.[19] In 2021, University of Cambridge student Talal Hangari was forcibly removed from his position as publicity officer of the Cambridge University Labour Club.[20] In 2022, Palestinian scholar and activist Shahd Abusalama of Sheffield

Hallam University was temporarily barred from teaching following a complaint about old social media posts.[21] Although she was fully exonerated by her university, the same group accused her again. After the third investigation, during which the university apparently engaged in covert communications with her accusers, she decided that she had to leave.[22] Alistair Hudson, head of the University of Manchester's art museum, was asked to leave his position following his efforts to resist censorship by the university, which preferred to yield to the pro-Israel UK Lawyers for Israel's request to remove a pro-Palestinian statement from its exhibition walls the previous year.[23]

Taken together, these cases of censorship demonstrate why the widespread tendency to trivialize free speech should be resisted. The stakes are much higher than the date and location of a controversial lecture. Someone who is denied the right to speak in a particular venue can still find a place to speak elsewhere. By contrast, those who are dismissed from employment are thereby rendered permanently unemployable. Take the case of Steven Salaita. After losing his job at the University of Illinois for posting tweets critical of Israel, Salaita obtained a visiting position at the American University in Beirut (AUB) as Edward W. Said chair of American studies. He accepted an offer that would have made this position permanent. That offer was abruptly rescinded by AUB president Fadlo Khuri, who alleged that procedural violations had made it necessary to cancel the search. Salaita emphasized that he left AUB against his will. Two years later, after an extended search for an academic position, Salaita announced that he was leaving academia permanently. He changed careers and became a bus driver in a suburb of Washington, DC. One unexpected side effect of this career transition is that Salaita's writing flourished. He began reaching a much wider public with reflections on life outside the academy on his blog. The fact that Salaita's most compelling reflections on academic freedom belong to the period after he severed his links to the academy is relevant to how we understand the role of universities in promoting free inquiry.

Soon after David Miller's comments became headlines, various governmental groups, including the All-Party Parliamentary Group Against Antisemitism, began calling for his dismissal. More than one hundred MPs signed a letter organized by this group. Speaking across party lines, in a rare show of unity, these MPs collectively informed the vice chancellor that Professor Miller had 'brought your university into disrepute'. They ended with the demand that the vice chancellor 'act now before any further damage is done'.[24] Miller's case rapidly became an international cause. Hundreds of academics signed a letter praising Miller as an 'eminent scholar' who was internationally known for his work on 'exposing the role that powerful actors and well-resourced, co-ordinated networks play in manipulating and stage-managing public debates, including on racism'.[25] Soon thereafter another letter circulated, partly in response to the first, condemning Miller's comments as 'the latest manifestation of a long and ignoble tradition of conspiracy theories concerning Jewish individuals and institutions'.[26] While this second letter did not call for Miller's dismissal, it made no mention of academic freedom. Yet surely the signatories knew that, in the absence of an explicit recognition of Miller's right to his views, the letter would be used to support calls for him to be fired.

The university finally issued a statement on 16 March 2021, confirming that an investigation was underway and refusing to comment further. Two Jewish professors at the University of Bristol, Tom Sperlinger and Gene Feder, wrote to the senior management as the investigation approached its end. They acknowledged the offence that had been caused, while expressing concern that the university might cave in to external pressures. Miller's dismissal, they argued, 'would create an extraordinarily dangerous precedent, if a campaign of this kind can lead to an academic – one of UoB's highest profile anti-racist scholars –

being sacked for legitimate work they have undertaken, and for their defence of it under duress'.[27]

These words proved prophetic. Three weeks later, the university announced that it was terminating Miller's employment on the grounds that he 'did not meet the standards of behaviour we expect from our staff'. This assessment relied on an unfortunate but familiar reframing of speech as 'behaviour', which is often used to evade the charge that academic freedom is being violated. When the termination was announced, many speculated about the reference in the university statement to an 'independent report' from a 'leading Queen's Counsel', whose name was withheld. According to the university statement, the QC report determined that 'Professor Miller's comments did not constitute unlawful speech'. Miller commented to the media that the report went further, clearing him of all charges of antisemitism.[28] His supporters asked why he had been terminated if the report had found no evidence of unlawful speech. His detractors wondered why the university statement made no reference to antisemitism as the reason for Miller's dismissal. In both cases, the reason was simple: the statement was not commissioned either to defend academic freedom or to combat antisemitism. Like every action taken by the university during these and related disputes, the report was commissioned in order to protect the institution in case of litigation, and especially judicial review. This bureaucratization of debate – which is commonplace rather than exceptional in such circumstances, and is entirely in keeping with my own experience – illustrates why we cannot trust universities, or any other institution, to protect free speech. Without a doubt, universities have a role to play, but a wider social transformation is needed.

As I followed these debates, I was struck that both sides seemed to regard the university's statement as a transparent reflection of what had in fact occurred, rather than as a political act in its own right. What was missed was how the university's statement was itself deeply political. The very way in which terms and concepts were formulated exerted institutional power over free speech, with the effect of undermining it. The statement opened by invoking the common-law concept of 'duty of care' as the principle that needed to be balanced against Miller's academic freedom. Those who are disturbed by the university's decision rightly wonder: What is the value of a 'duty of care' when it becomes the means by which free discussion is suppressed? In a context where free speech is suppressed, 'duty of care' is merely another tool in the armoury of power for crushing dissent.

My own experience in negotiating with the university four years earlier taught me to read university statements through a sceptical lens. I came to understand how university statements are worded not to ensure accuracy or out of a naive desire to represent the truth, but to minimize the risk to the university in case of litigation. Exposure to the judicial process taught me that in such circumstances universities tend to fear litigation more than anything else. Indeed, fear of judicial review seems to have been the primary motivation behind such investigations in my case, since the university had already informed me that they did not consider further action necessary, and this position changed only when its legal exposure became evident. A similar dynamic was likely at work in the case of the complaints against Miller. While a disgruntled employee can challenge any university decision at an employment tribunal with a minimum of expense, and without even hiring a lawyer, costly litigation such as judicial review is affordable only for groups with large cash reserves. Universities are well aware of this economic calculus. In the case of Miller, they conducted a cost–benefit analysis and decided in favour of Miller's complainants, and in deference to the legal threat they posed.

In both my case and Miller's, the most influential external organization was the Campaign Against Antisemitism. I observed first-hand the impact of the CAA's activities on the university's approach to my article. Initially I was told that my article did not require any kind of investigation, and even the university's lawyer told me that she had found nothing unacceptable in what I had written. But once the CAA made a complaint threatening legal action, a formal inquiry was a fait accompli. In Miller's case, the university commissioned a QC to inquire into the allegations against Miller. This was clearly designed to forestall further litigation by the CAA. The university aimed to show the world – as well as a potential court – that they had not harboured an antisemite on campus since 2018.

In August 2021, as the university investigation into Miller's comments dragged on, the CAA publicly announced that it was initiating legal proceedings against the university. It issued a public call to Jewish students at Bristol University to join its lawsuit against the university. Two months later, Bristol University officially terminated Miller's position, even before he had a chance to appeal. Although the university claimed not to have had any knowledge of the lawsuit when the *Bristol Tab* solicited a statement from it in August, its prior exchanges with the CAA in connection with my article make this doubtful. The university would certainly have factored the CAA response into their proceedings. Such pressures would also have encouraged them to hire a QC to produce an independent report, so that the university could show that it had shown due diligence if the case came to trial.

This sequence of events suggests that the university's insistence that Miller's words were not unlawful was motivated not by a desire to defend Miller or record the truth, but rather to protect itself from litigation by outside organizations. In line with these calculations, Miller's sacking was simply the collateral damage imposed by the university's need to protect itself from allegations of institutional antisemitism – a charge the CAA had reinforced in connection with evidence submitted to the Equality and Human Rights Commission in 2020. All of this evidence suggests that the university did not perceive firing Miller as posing a legal risk comparable to that posed by external organizations or by government threats. The ease with which his position was terminated demonstrates the weakness of legal protections for free speech within liberal democracies.

A Weak Framework for Free Speech

The UK has a weak legal framework when it comes to the defence of free speech, and this framework becomes more fragile with every violation of academic freedom. A measure of this weakness can be gleaned by the University of Birmingham's Free Speech Code of Practice, which mirrors that of many other universities across the UK.[29] Although the document recognizes that 'freedom of speech is a key part of the higher education experience' and 'respectful debate enables us to challenge discrimination, intolerance and harmful attitudes', this nominal recognition has minimal value when measured against the work the document does in practice. Like many such documents, the university's Free Speech Code of Practice is in fact a tool for suppressing freedom of speech, rather than enhancing it.[30] It exists in order to ensure that the university avoids risky topics and thoroughly complies with government regulations. The speech code mandates that anyone hoping to organize an event, whether online or in the classroom, follow internal procedures and obtain approval from management. It was invoked in 2022, when I proposed to deliver an inaugural lecture on the topic of free speech, and the outcome of the risk assessment was a recommendation that I include a chair with a perspective different from mine to avoid the perception of bias. I was also asked to demonstrate that 'a balanced range of views' would be shared.[31] Such procedural requirements considerably limit academics' freedom to arrange talks spontaneously with external speakers, since permission for any events they organize may be withheld by the university administration.

One of the key examples in the Equality and Human Rights Commission's misleadingly titled handbook, *Freedom of Expression:*

A Guide for Higher Education Providers and Students' Unions in England and Wales (2019), is a hypothetical scenario involving a 'high-risk speaker' who is said to have 'a history of associating with violent extremists and making statements that could risk drawing people into terrorism'.[32] Predictably, and in line with the institutional Islamophobia that has cast its spell over British universities, this 'high-risk speaker' who associates with 'violent extremists' is cast implicitly as Muslim in the hypothetical scenario. In such cases, we are told, the Prevent coordinator who is tasked with implementing Prevent legislation on UK university campuses must be consulted. The extremist speaker is given permission to speak on campus provided they 'agree to appear alongside another speaker with an alternative viewpoint', in order to provide a balanced perspective on whatever issues happen to be addressed. Notably, these calls for censorship occur in a government-sponsored document that is explicitly dedicated to the principle of free speech, and is posted as an authoritative guide to the subject on UK university websites.

Let us leave aside for a moment the logical fallacy entailed in the idea that 'balance' needs to be observed when implementing free speech; that point is taken up later in this chapter. For now, we can simply note how the EHRC's morality tale of a Muslim radical whose views must be 'balanced' by a British speaker illustrates a broader problem in the understanding of academic freedom across UK universities, and of freedom of speech more generally within British society. The demand that university academics treat controversial speakers as if they were guilty until proved innocent by actively soliciting other speakers to provide 'alternative viewpoints' reveals how entrenched Islamophobia has become within British universities. It also exposes a tendency within the UK to refuse to take free speech seriously on its own terms. Far from being havens for the expression of critical and dissenting views, universities police speech even more heavily than it is it is policed outside their walls.

The administrative requirement to install chairs to counter controversial views reached a peak of absurdity in 2017, when Cambridge University's director of communications was installed as a 'neutral' chair in order to counter the presumed bias of Palestinian academic Dr Ruba Salih. The occasion was the event 'BDS and the Globalised Struggle for Human Rights', co-hosted by Cambridge University's Palestine Society and its Middle East Society. Salih had no record of making controversial statements. She was of Palestinian origin and had extensive research experience relating to Palestinian refugees. One would think that this background would have made her an ideal person to chair a panel discussing Palestine.

The university's Prevent Referral Group thought otherwise. Presumably alerted to the event by someone unhappy with its anticipated criticism of Israel, this group, which was formed in line with UK anti-terrorism legislation and is chaired by Cambridge University president Stephen Toope, convened a meeting just a day prior to the event and determined that Salih should not be permitted to chair it. The group of non-experts unilaterally decided that the role of chair should go to someone else who could be relied on to neutralize the event's political undertones. Cambridge University apologized the following year after a lengthy inquiry into its handling of the affair, and acknowledged that 'there was no evidence to support the view that [Salih] would not ensure a democratic debate, allowing all views to be expressed'.[33] But the damage was done: the presumption of guilt lingers for the many who never saw this belated apology.

Complaints can be taken seriously without violating free speech. Internal complaints only compromise freedom of expression within a university context when they are handled badly. All complaints that originate with members of the university community deserve a fair and impartial hearing. Members of the university community with grievances should be allowed to disrupt everyday routines on their campus. As scholar-activists like Sara Ahmed have argued, space and attention must be given to such grievances, in order to challenge entrenched racism and sexism.[34] I have already argued that the historic failure on the part of universities to attend to the grievances of vulnerable members of the community has fostered inequality, resentment, and fear. Far from suppressing free speech, complaints and grievances are ways in which students and staff activate the potential of free speech to undo forced silences and expose suppressed histories.

As the examples of the suppression of pro-Palestinian speech and activism detailed throughout this book demonstrate, the greatest risk to free speech in university contexts comes not from internal debate, dissent, and complaint, but rather from external organizations and pressure groups that turn individuals into targets of proxy conflicts. Firing Miller was the university's response to this risk. We have every reason to expect that universities will cave in to pressure again, just as we can expect brave acts of resistance and non-compliance, such as occurred when the University of Aberdeen refused to adopt the IHRA definition and expressed concern over the 'recent high-profile cases which had resulted in academics losing their jobs', which suggested that 'the definition had become "weaponised" in the sector'.[35]

While Miller's supporters blame what happened to him on the Israel lobby, we should not ignore the more local and internal weaknesses that underlie free-speech violations. At best, existing free-speech regulations fail to safeguard free speech and academic freedom; at worst, they significantly undermine it.

If the stories of suppression and censorship documented in this book have anything to teach us, it is that, in their bureaucratic affairs, including in their management of conflict, universities easily succumb to external pressures to suppress academic freedom. In liberal democracies, every institution embraces the banner of free speech, but few consistently implement it. Most frequently, free speech is 'balanced' out of existence. Although universities are often idealized as places of free inquiry, the sordid history of the IHRA definition's implementation illustrates that universities all too often become the battleground of the proxy wars waged by the states that fund them.

Regardless of what you think of free speech as a means of achieving global solidarity in the fight against inequality, it is impossible to deny that, when it comes to defending those under fire for their views, leftist mobilization often fails to achieve its end. In recent years, the response of traditionally leftist organizations to crackdowns on free speech has sometimes done more harm than good. This is partly because, unlike socialists from earlier generations, contemporary leftists tend not to regard free speech as a value in itself. The honourable mandate of protecting and promote minority rights has become conflated with the view that it is legitimate, even necessary, to suppress offensive views. My experience of being attacked for my criticism of Israel has taught me that free speech must be defended; in its absence, we cannot credibly or seriously support the struggles of oppressed peoples around the world.

As Hangari noted, the contemporary left is often only willing to defend the right of others to speak out in the rare cases in which it can defend 'their each and every utterance'. No one on earth is so immune to error that every word they say ought to be defended. We should not need to defend the content of a person's words in order to defend their right to express them. Those who disagree with the statements of David Miller should understand that, far from being a case where the free speech argument falls apart, the controversy around Miller demonstrates the importance of free speech precisely because his views are controversial. Not least among the dangers of suppressing even reprehensible views is that it makes it easier for our opponents to use those same tactics against us.

Like freedom itself, free speech is a slippery concept. No single person, institution, or party has control over it. In the struggle to make Palestine visible, we must not surrender freedom of expression. We must learn to deploy it in ways that promote an egalitarian agenda, and that serve the ends of Palestinian liberation. Most urgently, we need to learn how to use free speech as a tactic against those who seek to silence us.

When my writings came under attack and outside groups began to call for my dismissal, I was advised to reframe the narrative that these groups were foisting on me as an attack on my academic freedom. At first, I resisted. Free speech, I believed, was for racists. Surely my ideas should be defended on their own terms, not according to free-speech principles. The more I tried to argue my case, however, the more clearly I came to perceive the intractability of disagreements over Israel and Zionism. I came to understand that, while the historical record unambiguously indicates that the history of Zionism is deeply entangled with the racism that besets many kinds of nationalism, it does not follow that every person who considers themselves Zionist is evil, or even racist. I learned that there is such a thing as irreconcilable disagreement, and that no amount of rational debate or human decency is going to resolve such conflicts.

As I began to revisit my own understanding of Jewish history and antisemitism, I came across an opinion piece by a woman who was a Holocaust survivor. She explained that, from her perspective, anti-Zionism was necessarily antisemitic because the denial of a Jewish homeland brought about the annihilation of her ancestors. From an objective perspective, the position seems logically indefensible, for no individual's story alone is enough to support such a dogmatic claim. Yet, from a subjective perspective, it is hard not to empathize with her point of view. Just as I am haunted by Leon's sympathy for the medieval antisemite while he wrote underground in Nazi-occupied Belgium, so did I feel it necessary to understand why a Holocaust survivor might believe that anti-Zionism is intrinsically antisemitic. Without accepting their logic, I want to see the matter from their perspective. Empathy does not equal agreement: all it requires is the recognition of another person's right to exist on their own terms as a thinking human being. All too often, we deny our fellow humans this recognition.

113

At the time when I was accused of antisemitism, I was accustomed to associating free-speech mobilization with right-wing and white-nationalist movements. I saw these prejudices compounded in the response to my article. Palestinian perspectives were systematically side-lined in the reactions against it. Since the erasure of Palestinians and of Palestine seemed to me like the greatest harm, I concluded that my counter-mobilization should centre Palestinian perspectives. At the same time, I had to think strategically. Why was it necessary to cede the freedoms that right-wing movements had appropriated for themselves, which they were using to harm the Palestinian cause? Why not reclaim these as well? Why surrender to my accusers the right to define the boundaries of my permissible speech?

The Inhumanity of Academic Freedom

Steven Salaita, the Palestinian-American professor best known for his abrupt 'dehiring' from the University of Illinois due to his outspoken criticisms of Israel, is also the author of a remarkable essay on academic freedom and its limits, entitled 'The Inhumanity of Academic Freedom'.[36] Appropriately, given the twinned history of Israeli and South African apartheid, the essay was first presented as the 2019 T. B. Davie Memorial Lecture on academic freedom at the University of Cape Town. This lecture series has a long history of inspiring scholars and activists such as Kenan Malik, Wole Soyinka, Noam Chomsky, and Edward Said to reflect on the scope and purpose of free speech. The parallel histories of apartheid and political struggle within Palestinian and South African universities are living testimony to the stakes of free speech within these respective societies' struggles for freedom.

Salaita does not aim, with his provocative title, to denigrate academic freedom as such. Rather, he situates the freedom specific to universities as a necessary condition for their flourishing within a wider context of freedoms that are just as important – or even more so. Salaita's point is that an exclusive focus on academic freedom that fails to recognize the barriers to achieving other freedoms cannot liberate silenced voices. As he writes, 'academic freedom is always conditional on a corresponding politics'. The same holds for free speech in general. In a world that has normalized white nationalism and global inequality, free speech is bound to come up short when it comes to protecting individuals who face systematic discrimination.

So far, so good. But why stop with this critique? Can we imagine another world in which the freedom to speak is understood to be intrinsic to anti-racist liberation? I want to persuade you – so that you can persuade others – that resisting definition-based approaches to antisemitism and centring Palestinian voices requires us to take free speech seriously, and not just when we happen to agree with the person under attack. It means rejecting the approach to freedom of expression that has been internalized within the UK, and is gaining traction within the United States even though it undermines the First Amendment.

As if by default, when academics speak, they are understood to represent the university. Every once in a while, an academic or their employer will come out and say that their views do not represent those of their university, but this only reinforces the assumption that the opposite holds if it is not explicitly stated otherwise. As a result, it is accepted that the speech of academics is regulated by the universities that employ them. By contrast with this established approach, my experience with free speech suggests that it is necessary to distinguish between workplace-specific utterances, such as those uttered in a classroom context, and utterances made outside the workplace, which the employer has no right to monitor, let alone punish. Whether the employee in question is a university professor or a bus driver, what they do and say on their own time, outside workplace contexts, is their own business.[37] The IHRA definition of antisemitism has taken hold of UK universities with such disastrous consequences partly because workplace protections for free speech are underdeveloped in British culture, society, and legal discourse generally.

At the end of his essay, Salaita insists that we must look beyond academic freedom to focus instead on 'simply freedom, una-dorned, unmediated, unmodified'. I agree. Free speech should always be situated within this broader understanding of free-dom. It is with Salaita's critique in mind that I want to probe the progressive potential of free speech to bring about political free-dom. Academic freedom can only be meaningful in a society that protects the free speech of all its citizens. When it is used only to shore up professional privilege and stifle the voices of those who are silenced by abuses of power, academic freedom loses its value in society at large. Such a devaluation of academic freedom – what Salaita calls its 'inhumanity' – happened when a number of Harvard University professors circulated a letter defending Harvard anthropologist John Comaroff when he was accused of sexual harassment in 2022.[38] Comaroff subsequently resumed teaching at Harvard, making the letter unnecessary, but not before this troubling use of academic freedom to protect abuses of power was exposed.

As Salaita notes, in its current form, academic freedom is 'incapable of preventing unsanctioned forms of punishment, reg-ulation of the job market according to docility, or the increasing contingency of labor'. These incapacities limit the utility of academic freedom as a value in itself. Instead of celebrating academic freedom in isolation from other forms of social justice, academic free speech should be woven into a wider conception of the freedoms that are central to our collective emancipation. Before I say more about the intersections of free speech and academic freedom with the wider pursuit of justice, it is neces-sary to dwell on the political significance of an even more basic value for democratic mobilization: freedom itself.

Who better to guide us on such a journey than Karl Marx? Marx's life and writings demonstrate his commitment to freedom of thought. He began his journalism career as the founder and editor of the *Rheinische Zeitung* (1842–43), a radical newspaper that was shut down by the Prussian state censor just over a year after its initial publication. The suppressed newspaper was revived by Marx and Engels six years later as the *Neue Rheinische Zeitung* (1848–49), until it too was shut down by the censors. During its brief existence, the *Neue Rheinische Zeitung* was among the most influential radical newspapers in western Europe.

Like his political theory, Marx's concept of press freedom – and hence of freedom of speech – was more radical than that of his liberal contemporary with whom the concept of free speech is most often associated today: utilitarian philosopher John Stuart Mill. Mill's *On Liberty* (1859) is perhaps the single most widely cited work on free speech in the world today. But Mill did not diagnose as perceptively as Marx, or even Salaita, the manifold ways in which free speech so often comes to be manipulated and turned into a handmaiden of power. Marx criticises the liberal-rights framework adopted by Mill on the grounds of its excessive focus on the individual. By contrast with the liberals of his era, Marx conceived of freedom of speech and freedom of the press as rights that were collective in substance and intersectional in their politics. For Marx, freedom of speech was under no obligation to be neutral. Rather, the point of free speech – and the reason why it had to be defended – was to undermine existing regimes of power.

Marx anticipates Salaita's complaint that 'rights pretend to be neutral entitlements disbursed according to need' when they are in actuality 'commodities managed by bureaucrats paid handsomely to indulge the ruling class under the guise of collective values'. Also like Salaita, Marx recognizes that free speech can mask unequal distributions of power, and that by itself it cannot rectify these inequities. Because Marx places power at the centre of his analysis, he is able to account for freedom of speech as a way of resisting state power more persuasively than can the conventional liberal separation between the public and private spheres. Free speech, for Marx, is not about balancing different points of view; it does not culminate in a celebration of individual autonomy or the restoration of private rights, which separate us from our wider communities. Rather, free speech, for Marx – like freedom itself – is collective.

Marx's controversial early essay 'On the Jewish Question' (1843) critically examines the ideology of private, liberal rights that in his view undermine genuine freedom of the press. Criticizing the clampdown on press freedom during the French Revolution, Marx wrote that, under this new revolutionary regime so often associated with progress, 'freedom of the press is completely destroyed'.[39] He criticized the French Revolution's subordination of 'human freedom' to 'public freedom', because it meant in practice the curtailment of press freedom whenever the press challenged political power. Within the constitution established by the French Revolution, 'the human right of freedom ceases to be a right as soon as it conflicts with *political* life'. Yet, according to the liberal tradition, political life is merely 'the guarantee of human rights, the rights of the individual man'. To such limited perspectives, Marx juxtaposes a vision of human freedom that is collective in that it demands justice and equality, and cherishes rather than suppresses the disagreements that inevitably arise between citizens.

Marx also objects to the separation of the social good from the rights of the individual. Unlike the leaders of the French Revolution and many who would later undertake revolution in his name, Marx is consistent in his defence of freedom – including freedom of speech – as a collective project intrinsic to revolutionary activity. As he writes in 'On the Jewish Question', only when the individual 'no longer separates the social force from himself . . . is human emancipation completed'.[40] Marx's belief that the cultural substratum of Jewish identity would eventually fade away is both objectionable and erroneous. But his early efforts at thinking through the relation between rights and identity remain relevant for a leftist approach to free speech; such an approach, protecting minority rights in a world dominated by censorious and coercive definitions, must conceive of the social and the political as one. His materialist understanding of free speech as intrinsic to the struggle for power inspired the journalistic and editorial endeavours of later materialists such as Abram Leon.

While Marx exposed the hypocrisy of liberal-rights regimes, he explicitly argued for free speech in his journalism. Perhaps anticipating the closure of his newspaper by the censors, Marx asserted in his first published article: 'The real, *radical cure for censorship* would be its *abolition*.'[41] The fact that this radical premise has never been taken up by any socialist government – including those that acted in Marx's name – means that free speech has yet to be formally implemented from a Marxist perspective. A leftist history of free speech has yet to be lived, let alone written. Whereas the last decades of the twentieth century witnessed a gradual bifurcation between free speech as a value and leftist politics, the twenty-first century may yet witness their realignment.[42]

In his insistence on the foundational status of free speech, Marx shares common ground with liberals like Mill. His departures from the liberal conception of free speech are exactly what make his work relevant to leftist politics. The concept of free speech that Marx defends does not rely on the 'marketplace of ideas' that heavily informs Mill's thinking, which is the focus of Salaita's critique. Marx does not entrust the regulation of free speech to the marketplace, or wager his commitment to equality on the naive hope that the best views will naturally prevail. But Marx is just as categorically opposed to imposing his convictions on others by force. During his editorship of the *Rheinische Zeitung* Marx instructed his contributors that they should avoid anything that might be read as propaganda. 'I regard it as inappropriate, indeed even immoral', he wrote, 'to smuggle communist and socialist doctrines, hence a new world outlook, into incidental theatre criticisms . . . I demand a quite different and more

119

thorough discussion of communism, if it should be discussed at all.'[43] The world's best-known communist believed that it should not be smuggled in through the back door by undermining free speech. Marx believed that ideas had to be argued for, rationally and dialectically, not imposed by fiat, if they were to bring about collective liberation. He placed his faith in the power of critique rather than the demands of the market.

Salaita correctly notes that the ideological defence of free speech falls short when it obscures actual relations of power. Although they are packaged by their proponents as 'neutral entitlements disbursed according to need', rights are often in practice 'commodities managed by bureaucrats'. Palestinians know better than most how a people's collective rights can be denied for decades through bureaucratic manipulations and liberal justifications.

Sleights of hand analogous to those documented above at the University of Bristol and across the UK have occurred in many North American and European universities. The rhetoric around free speech and 'cancel culture' circulated by the UK's Conservative government since the adoption of the IHRA definition illustrates just how contingent and subject to manipulation rights discourses can be. When politicians bemoan 'cancel culture' on free-speech grounds, they often paper over differentials of power between those who are silenced by campaigns to de-platform a speaker and by liberal bureaucrats who either enforce or reject cancellation. Yet anyone familiar with Palestinian activism in Europe and North America knows that it is singled out for censorship far more frequently than any other form of dissent. This singling-out points to the need to develop an approach to free speech that is specifically suited to advancing Palestinian freedom and working for the liberation of other marginalized peoples.

Against Balance

Indian philosopher Akeel Bilgrami has dedicated his energies to carving out a space for Palestinian activism within the free-speech tradition. It is no accident that Bilgrami's thinking about free speech was developed at Columbia University in New York City, an educational institution that has at various times been the target of crackdowns on freedom to dissent in relation to Palestine. Bilgrami developed his critique of Mill's notion of free speech at a time when the lives and careers of political scientist Norman Finkelstein and anthropologist Nadia Abu El-Haj, as well as Steven Salaita, were coming under intense attack from Israel advocacy groups, in each case due to their writings about Israel. While El-Haj was eventually granted tenure, Finkelstein was banished from the academy forever. Alongside his academic pursuits, Bilgrami has been outspoken in defence of Finkelstein.[44]

Bilgrami's defence of wilful imbalance begins with a critique of Mill. Mill presents several arguments as to why democratic states should tolerate ideas that we abhor, focusing on the most influential among them. Mill's proposal to 'tolerate dissenting opinions just in case our current opinions are wrong and these dissenting opinions are right' continues to dominate liberal understandings of academic freedom.[45] As Bilgrami notes, this argument, which relies on the notion of balance as a hedge against the possibility of being wrong, is incoherent even on its own terms. It is premised on the belief that there is an Archimedean point from which we can accurately assess intractable conflicts, and on a denial of the role of human subjectivity in constituting our most basic beliefs. Yet, no matter how incoherent it is, this fiction is influential in our political present because 'imbalance' is frequently the basis on which university teachers and Palestine activists are smeared as antisemitic. More generally, 'balance' is a staple of university free-speech codes, and I have myself been encouraged by university administrators to display balance in my engagements with this issue. The call for balance is also a means of silencing dissident voices and marginalizing non-majoritarian views. Consider the case of Ruba Salih, an anthropologist who was presumed to lack 'balance' because she was Palestinian. Salih was removed as chair of a BDS event at Cambridge University. The solution to such imbalance, this argument tends to run, is to artificially impose a more 'even-handed' paradigm, so that students will be exposed to both the Israeli and Palestinian sides. The problem with such approaches is that they assume an unerring capacity to locate the middle ground, often without leaving the matter open to debate.

As Bilgrami rightly argues, few topics in the humanities are well served by such artificial balancing acts. Here is why: any classroom instructor ought to make an effort not just to be reasonably informed about the subjects they plan to teach, but also to decide, among an overwhelming mass of materials, evidence, and claims, which narratives are most persuasive and which details most worth presenting to students. Selectivity can generate bias – but it is also epistemologically necessary, and not in itself problematic. Provided that the material has been judiciously selected, it would be silly to insist that all sides of a given issue be given equal treatment. Do we demand that proponents of the hypothesis that the earth is flat have a place in a classroom context? Not at all. So, too, with those who whitewash Israel's crimes or suppress key facts about the Nakba, the Holocaust, or related atrocities for political ends. All ideas and arguments are not equally valid, and no responsible teacher or scholar would pretend they are.

Balance is not the most important criterion of selection, especially in cases where the middle ground is itself contested. Rather, criteria such as accuracy and depth should guide us. A good instructor will be humble, open-minded, and honest in recognizing areas of confusion and doubt. But she will also have reached certain conclusions based on evidence available to her.

Her responsibility as a teacher is to communicate those conclusions – and the point of view that informs them – as effectively as possible, not to seek to represent all sides and all points of view. Being able to exercise the principle of selectivity is part of good teaching, research, and thinking. If we cannot venture at least a tentative conclusion regarding the issue at hand that goes beyond the mechanical requirement for balance, then, Bilgrami asks, what business do we have being in a classroom in the first place?

Instructors are obliged to be informed about the subjects they teach, but it would be foolish to expect them to have no opinion whatsoever. Bilgrami attributes the 'constant demand that we always present both sides of a disagreement' to a 'conception of education as a sort of chronic dithering'.[46] Far from being objective or neutral, the instructor who is beholden to a mechanical concept of balance on any issue, including Israel/Palestine, undermines her own credibility in the classroom. Teaching well requires conviction, and conviction requires taking sides.

Bilgrami goes even further than these claims in pursuit of a more expansive foundation for academic freedom. He acknowledges the absolute value of a diversity of viewpoints, perspectives, and backgrounds in the university environment. For Bilgrami, this is the most compelling argument for academic freedom. But intellectual diversity by itself is inadequate in clarifying the responsibility of the intellectual, which is to speak truth to power, sometimes at great personal risk. The intellectual who speaks truth to power must consider not only the content of what needs to be said, but the context in which it will be heard and potentially acted upon. Free speech only acquires meaning in relation to an audience, which in turn implies a political community and context. Far from catering to what that audience may wish to hear, the committed intellectual, activist, and disinterested scholar should focus their criticism precisely on what those in power are least likely to want to hear. In this sense, academic freedom is inseparable from freedom in general.

Isaac Deutscher, the self-described 'non-Jewish Jew', insisted that his identity obliged him to adhere to a certain kind of partiality. In Deutscher's own words: 'I am . . . a Jew by force of my unconditional solidarity with the persecuted and exterminated.' What Bilgrami sees as the task of the intellectual is what Deutscher connects with his identity as a Jew. It is impossible to legislate how this solidarity with the persecuted ought to be justified at the individual level. Those who impose a phantom notion of objectivity onto what Bilgrami calls 'wilful imbalance' often conceal political motivations beneath the cloak of impartiality. Instead of ceding to their demands, we should focus on how we can use wilful imbalance – what Deutscher calls 'unconditional solidarity with the persecuted' – to advance the freedom of all oppressed peoples.

Bilgrami's critique of Mill brings us full circle. Salaita's criticisms of the concept of academic freedom are justified as a critique of historical and contemporary liberalism, including John Stuart Mill and the Anglo-American approach to free speech that he inspired. Leftists who see beyond the liberal emphasis on balance can contemplate different – more democratic and more radical – foundations for free speech. This concept of free speech is an extension of freedom itself, applied to the sphere of language, and no leftist politics can do without it. Marx, Luxemburg, and Trotsky each developed different leftist approaches to and justifications for free speech. For each thinker, the Marxian dream of abolishing censorship was foundational to the struggle for equality.

Whatever viewpoint one takes, it is important to recognize that the need for free speech is as instinctual as it is intellectual. It is necessary not just to democratic flourishing, but more fundamentally to human existence. Free speech gives voice to views that political authorities would like to supress. For those who practice and encourage it, it helps us come to terms with ourselves, in our relation to others. When my own voice was silenced and my views were censored, I felt that my ability to exist as a human being was also under threat. In the scheme of things, the censorship I experienced was minor; many worse instances of suppression, particularly of Palestinians, have been documented in this chapter. Classical justifications of free speech drawn from the liberal tradition obscure what it really means to silence another person's voice. It is a denial, through the language of moderation and balance, of their right to exist.

Materialism and the Reservoir Theory

I will end this chapter where it began, with the case of David Miller. We can now explore it from the much broader context opened up by a materialist approach to free speech that I have endeavoured to outline. David Feldman is perhaps the most frequently cited scholar of contemporary antisemitism in this book. Feldman has been a major participant in the debate around the IHRA definition and a major influence on me personally. His approach to understanding antisemitism illuminates many aspects of the issue. Among his most important insights is that we can be antisemitic without intending to be, and without knowing that we are. Seemingly neutral stereotypes about Jews and money can, for example, become the foundation for insidious conspiracies.[47] Such stereotypes may be mixed with philosemitism and promoted by Jews themselves. This does not make them any less pernicious, but it does clarify how antisemitism can be normalized and pass unquestioned. On Feldman's account, culpability is social before it is individual. Antisemitism does not require conscious or deliberate hatred of any specific group; it is absorbed by osmosis and permeates our cultural reservoirs.[48] Within this framework, antisemitism can be understood as a reservoir of prejudice we inherit by virtue of membership in modern society. Antisemitic prejudice is as fluid, as malleable, as subject to change, and as ubiquitous as water.

Another advantage of Feldman's approach, and of his scholarship on antisemitism generally, is what – for lack of a better term – might be called its methodological objectivity. In a polemical atmosphere where most commentators tend to sort themselves into anti- and pro-Zionist factions, Feldman consistently positions his interventions above the fray (with a single exception, discussed below). As a result, his reflections and insights must be reckoned with regardless of one's political position. Feldman's ability to navigate highly contentious political issues without compromising on the objectivity of his insights, generating work that no participant in this debate can afford to ignore, calls to mind the work of another similarly gifted historian of a very different period, Arnaldo Momigliano.

Known primarily as an historian of antiquity who migrated first to the UK and then to the United States amid the Nazi genocide that killed both of his parents, Momigliano was gifted with an ability to distil, in scintillating prose, lessons from the distant past for use in the present. The pasts that most engaged Momigliano were those of Jews, ancient Romans, and Greeks – but eventually his expertise expanded to encompass the entire world.[49] I discovered Momigliano's work in 2008, when I was a PhD student at Columbia University. While Momigliano's research had nothing directly to teach me on the subject of my PhD research, his way of relating to the past shook me to the core. During those heady years, under Momigliano's influence, I drafted a manuscript on antiquarian philology, which I hope will eventually see the light of day. Although I could not find a way to connect Momigliano's historiography to my own research, I distilled the inspiration I took from his method and style into an article exploring the ongoing relevance of his historical method.[50]

These reflections have a similar relationship to the work of Feldman as those earlier pages from my graduate school years did to the work of Momigliano. I write as someone from an empirically distant world from that of Feldman, with a different kind of expertise, who from time to time finds herself moving in directions that would have been alien to the source of her inspiration, and yet who nonetheless turns to that scholar as a compass for orientating her own views. I trust the direction in which Feldman is travelling, even when there are certain detours that I have been compelled to make from his path. Like Momigliano's work, Feldman's writing on antisemitism is marked by integrity even when his polemical pieces lead him to conclusions I find problematic.

To its credit, the conceptualization of antisemitism and other forms of prejudice as 'a deep reservoir of stereotypes and narratives, replenished over time, and from which people can draw with ease, whether they intend to or not' awakens us to its ubiquity across time and space, and reveals how many of us are complicit in propagating this prejudice in our thinking and in our lives.[51] Yet when we try to use the reservoir theory as a guide to inform what we do about specific cases of antisemitism that involve controversial anti-Zionists who have been persecuted for their views, its limits become evident.

Anti-Zionism today is entangled in many different political agendas; consensus will never be reached with regard to when the border into antisemitism is crossed. As much as I contest how Israel's advocates have drawn this border, I do not think any honest person could deny that there is at least an occasional association – which is far from being causal – between anti-Zionism and antisemitism. The two sometimes occur together – just as antisemitism has accompanied a wide range of other tropes throughout time and space – even though analytically they are completely distinct. In short, the reservoir theory leaves matters of agency and culpability unresolved. The famous question first posed by Russian revolutionary Nikolai Chernyshevsky and subsequently by Lenin – *What Is to be Done?* – is one that the reservoir theory of antisemitism by itself does not answer.

To say that the practical implications of the reservoir theory are unclear is less a criticism of the theory than a commentary on the near impossibility of defining antisemitism once and for all. Feldman refers to the need for education, and this is a goal that I share, but educational institutions are, as I have shown, often implicated in supressing freedom and preventing debate. A rigorous commitment to free speech, by contrast, offers a clear programme, which is to permit offensive and problematic speech, even – especially – when we are opposed to its contents. One implication of taking free speech seriously is that it enables us to distinguish between words and actions.[52] Another implication is that it prevents us from advocating the punishment of anyone for what they say in their own private capacity, whether on social media or elsewhere. These proposals will not appeal to many, but at least they have a degree of transparency that can be applied anywhere. They offer a way out of the dead-end of silence and suppression to which the IHRA definition – like other group-specific definitions of racism – leads.

The absence of a clear programme within the reservoir theory of antisemitism, or in most of the recent attempts to control the damage wrought by the IHRA definition, opens up a gap that is further exposed in Feldman's writings about the case of David Miller. In my view, the utility of the reservoir theory is not to be found in the calls to terminate Miller's employment. Instead, I think the reservoir theory is most useful as a means of recognizing and understanding the ubiquity of antisemitism, not litigating against it. When it comes to political implementation, the materialism of Abram Leon offers a necessary supplement to the reservoir theory's descriptive role. Specifically, Leon's dialectical materialism provides us with a framework for intersectional solidarity that the reservoir theory arguably lacks. Like the reservoir theory, it recognizes the contingency of human prejudice, but it also locates specific instances of antisemitism within a wider socioeconomic framework. Had the reservoir theory been able to incorporate a materialist analysis into its framework, the dangers of terminating Miller's employment would have been clear.

Feldman describes antisemitism as a reservoir of prejudices from which discourses 'flood in from time to time', depending on the narratives most active in a specific political juncture.[53] In its discursive orientation, the reservoir theory has limited political purchase; it does not tell us what we should do about this inheritance, aside from educating ourselves and others. It tells us that antisemitism is everywhere, and sensitizes us to its ubiquity, but does not give us the political tools to eradicate it. At worst, recognizing the ubiquity of antisemitism might even serve as an impediment to action.

The difficulty of the reservoir argument is intrinsic to its discursive orientation. Antisemitism is not going to go away anytime soon, no matter how many definitions we formulate to describe it, how much we legislate against it, or how many professors we fire or activists we ban in order to keep it on the margins of society. Discursive change alone cannot form a solution to dealing with any kind of racism. Meanwhile, the collateral damage done when the struggle against antisemitism is appropriated by xenophobic and Islamophobic political agendas that also undermine freedom of speech may contribute to a net increase in antisemitism around the world, as well as racism more broadly. Such substitutions, whereby xenophobic political agendas, Islamophobic policies, and anti-Palestinian sentiment are wrapped up into right-wing crusades against antisemitism, have the effect of suppressing pro-Palestinian speech and freedom of inquiry in general.

A case in point is the recent claim of right-wing commentator and former *New York Times* columnist Bari Weiss that a growing Muslim population makes it 'dangerous to be a Jew in Europe'.[54] In this passage, Weiss omits the more direct impact of Europe's long history of antisemitism on contemporary Jews. Such dichotomies are not good for Jews, or indeed for anyone, yet many pro-Israel advocates are willing to subordinate legitimate concerns about the suppression of human rights and civil liberties that are entailed in their crusades against antisemitism in order to promote their political agendas. This is no better – and of course no worse – than left-wing anti-Zionists who propagate antisemitic stereotypes in the name of supporting Palestinian rights. Needless to say, both types of misappropriation must be contested in the strongest possible terms.

The limits of the reservoir approach are exposed when we try to use it to construct a plan for shifting the cultural foundations of antisemitic prejudice. At that point, it becomes apparent that the political implications of acknowledging antisemitism's ubiquity have not been accounted for. This is not to say that the reservoir approach excludes politics, but simply that, left to fend for itself in a politically fraught environment, an approach to antisemitic discourse that sees it simply as a reservoir of society's prejudice may fall into errors of political judgement when its political stance is inconsistent or unarticulated. The use of the Jerusalem Declaration on Antisemitism (JDA) to justify the termination of Miller's employment (see below) is arguably one such error.[55]

After demonstrating the ubiquity of antisemitism, the reservoir theory inclines in one of two directions: on one hand, a kind of fatalism, whereby antisemitism's ubiquity may lead to apathy concerning the possibility of overcoming it; on the other, a moralism that suppresses the political lessons of this ubiquity and mistakes effects for causes. If combined with a materialist approach, the reservoir theory could more effectively advance the struggle for equality and social justice. But such a meeting of methods has yet to happen.

Recent history has shown that definitions of antisemitism set in motion political processes that subsequently acquire a will of their own, becoming mixed up in issues that have nothing to do with fighting racism and everything to do with amassing political capital. Government adoption of any definition of antisemitism has political, not just intellectual, consequences. Managing these issues well requires more than simply getting antisemitism right; we also need to reckon with ourselves. We need to grasp the political context within which antisemitism is adjudicated and forged, including within our minds and hearts. We need to ask questions, not only about what statements, perceptions, and actions we consider antisemitic, but also what we consider to be the appropriate response to it. We need to figure out what our position really is – not what we tell ourselves we believe, but what we actually believe, in the deepest chambers of our minds and hearts – on the legitimate scope of human freedom.

The firing of David Miller brings into focus the political stakes in our approach to antisemitism and its eradication. It matters not because so many academics are outraged, but precisely because they are not. Many cannot bring themselves to oppose the firing of someone whose ideas they find abhorrent. Although he has commented on the matter extensively, Feldman has not publicly recognized Bristol's firing of Miller as a violation of academic freedom. At the same time, both Feldman and Yair Wallach have cogently shown how Miller's work perpetuates antisemitic stereotypes.[56] I fully accept their critiques, but I fear that free speech falls by the wayside in their analysis. Particularly concerning is their use of the JDA in support of their case against Miller, as it lends weight to the argument that the JDA could become as troublesome as the IHRA definition in suppressing free speech. By contrast, a materialist approach to antisemitism may be more effective than the reservoir theory in reconciling the conflicting claims of free speech and antisemitism, because it focuses on the wider context within which academics and other workers are vulnerable to exploitation and censorship under capitalism. This context too is relevant to understanding Bristol's firing of Miller, but the reservoir theory takes no account of it.

My reservations about the reservoir theory – or, rather, my desire to supplement it with Leon's dialectical materialism – stem not from disagreement with its approach to the concept of antisemitism or its presence in our society, but rather from a different understanding of the legitimate place of free speech in a democratic society. Since these divergences correlate with differences between British and American approaches to free speech generally, they likely also reflect the differences of the cultures that have formed me, as an American who migrated the UK. The biggest difference between those who support Miller's firing and my own is the First Amendment of the US Constitution, not the definition of antisemitism. According to the First Amendment, all speech that does not directly foster crime is protected speech. Importantly, this protection extends to racist speech – a standard that seems unthinkable in the UK.

Why protect racist speech? We tend to assume that free speech exists in order to protect the views of those we agree with. Since few people are consciously racist by their own admission, the prevalent view is that obviously misguided speech, including racist speech, ought to be censured rather than protected. As First Amendment jurisprudence recognizes, definitions of racism are subjective. Not all definitions of racism are created equal; some are better and some are worse. Although racism has not adequately been defined for legal purposes – since any legal definition would need to be cognizant of its implementation, and this has not occurred – this does not mean it cannot be defined at all. While definitions can be debated endlessly, there is no reason to expect that the conflict among different definitions will ever be resolved. In a context of debates that do not lead to resolution, the only approach consistent with human freedom is to reserve judgement from the point of view of the law and let people decide on their own. This is one reason why even racist speech is protected under the First Amendment, but it is not necessarily the most important one.

A more important reason for including racist speech within the category of speech protected under the First Amendment is that any speech-based regulation inevitably augments the power of the state, and therefore of bureaucrats who implement the state's regulations. Since states are known to abuse their power, it should not be granted lightly. Further, a thought is not the same as an act. Thankfully, institutionalized racism has long been established as illegal within both UK and US jurisprudence, and it is worth looking into ways to develop this legislation further. But thought cannot be policed, not even by the self (as Freud well understood). In no case should a thought in itself be conflated

132

with culpability. Racist speech is and should be protected by free-speech laws not because it is valid in any way, but because policing it cannot be made consistent with democratic governance.[57] This doesn't mean that there shouldn't be any consequences for racist speech; rather it means that the standard for criminal punishment such as imprisonment is not met by racist speech alone. There are, however, numerous ways to counter and resist racist speech that do not violate human freedom.

Quoting the 2010 Equality Act, Feldman states that Miller's criticisms of Jewish students at the University of Bristol, which amounted to criticism of their attacks on him, constituted 'unwanted conduct that has the purpose or effect of creating an intimidating, hostile, degrading or offensive environment' that violated the dignity of Jewish students. The evidence in the public domain, which Miller has personally corroborated as the reason for his dismissal, makes the accusation of harassment seem far-fetched.[58] The claim that Miller's case does not involve academic freedom because he was accused of harassing students either misses or rejects the necessity of protecting racist speech within a free-speech framework. In addition, Feldman's implicit defence of the campaign to get Miller fired evades this movement's political intent.

Miller's firing illustrates the stakes of free speech – not because his views are beyond criticism but precisely because few are willing to defend them. This important aspect of the free-speech case against Miller's firing has been missed by most participants in the debate. The axiom attributed to Voltaire – 'I disapprove of what you say, but I will defend to the death your right to say it' – captures the attitude that is needed, even though few have been willing to adopt it.[59]

Defenders of free speech and academic freedom ought not to be in the business of defending only ideas they like – and yet the controversy around Miller has overwhelmingly taken the form of two sides battling against each other, one side defending Miller's ideas while the other condemns them. Whatever happened to the imperative to defend someone's right to say what we in fact condemn? When someone claims that a controversy around an idea that they (rightly or wrongly) despise has no bearing on academic freedom, that claim should be examined closely. Changing the conversation from academic freedom to harassment in the analysis of Miller's firing distracts us from the wider political context of administrative power and employment precarity that has overdetermined the outcome of these events. It is not persuasive to claim that complaining about someone else's criticisms, even if that someone else happens to be a student, is in itself a form of harassment. Further, this deflection does little to advance our understanding of either antisemitism or academic freedom. It also fails to take account of the arguments made by the anonymous QC who was tasked to provide an opinion on Miller's case and determine whether he had been guilty of harassment. In that report, which Feldman later criticized, the QC argued that, according to the Equality Act 2010, Miller could only be 'guilty of "harassment" or "discrimination"' in a case in which 'he is acting as an employee of the University'. Importantly, the QC insisted that acting as an employee of a university 'would not readily extend . . . to participation in a conference, the writing of articles, or the provision of quotes to journalists'.[60] The position is further clarified in terms that ought to resonate with anyone who cares about protecting the autonomy and integrity of intellectual inquiry from political interference:

> There is an element to the role of academics as public intellectuals that sits uneasily in my view with the idea that outward facing work of the sort at issue here is performed *for the University as employer* . . . the protection of academic freedom . . . must entail that academics are not to be seen as the mouthpieces of the institutions by which they are employed.[61]

Feldman's analysis does not distinguish between the public intellectual speaking in their own capacity and the academic speaking

as a university employee. Yet academics must, like workers anywhere, be allowed to function as private individuals, not as
representatives of their employer, even when they make public
statements, present their research in public fora outside the university, and publish articles with their university affiliations.
Teaching is different: it is addressed to a specific group of students, not to the general public. What is said in the classroom is
subject to different standards than what is said in the public
sphere. Academics require the freedom *not* to represent their universities outside classroom contexts. Because the only valid
charge ever made against Miller pertained to his extramural
statements in non-university contexts, his firing in effect denies
this freedom to all academics, setting a dangerous precedent. In
the end, the university acted against Miller and contrary to the
conclusions of the report it had commissioned. Hence, the rejection of the employee's right not to be treated as a representative
of their university is enshrined in the university's decision. This
outcome undermines the freedom of all academics, as well as the
integrity of the profession to which they belong.

While it can substantiate the argument that Miller's work is
embedded in numerous conspiracy theories that are antisemitic
in their exposition if not in their intent, the reservoir theory does
not confront the paradox that follows from this analysis: the
body of work that was found to be problematic in 2021 was
vetted by numerous scholarly associations, journals, and even
funders, including the UK-government funded Economic and
Social Research Council (ESRC) over the course of many years.
Such a long list of approvals does not make Miller's work immune
to Feldman's critique; it does, however, mean that, to the extent
that it is problematic, any problems were embedded within the
entire academic culture that had supported it for decades. Due
process matters, and even anti-racism does not justify its violation. It matters that Miller was hired into a permanent position
at the University of Bristol even when the work that Feldman and
others have found problematic was already published. Whatever

one's views on the validity of the hiring committee's assessment, it should have been regarded as irreversible on speech-related grounds.

Feldman implicitly acknowledges that Miller's problematic work long pre-dates the moment when he began to be accused of antisemitism.[62] Miller did not undergo a sudden 'antisemitic transformation' on his arrival at the University of Bristol in 2019. His work was consistently problematic in precisely the ways Feldman describes. Any charge of antisemitism directed against Miller would also need to be directed against the academic institutions that supported Miller's work, including the ESRC. And perhaps this is exactly where the reservoir theory leads us, in the realm of ideas, given its aim to reveal how antisemitic prejudice permeates an entire society in more or less unconscious ways. At its best, such an approach has its merits: it shares the contextual emphasis of materialism, and reminds us that, as we know from decades of critical race theory, racism is first and foremost structural. Understood contextually, it could even limit the impulse to make individuals like Miller into targets when they merely illustrate a wider phenomenon. Even legitimate critiques cannot target someone for their beliefs without violating freedom of speech.

In short, we require a much more nuanced account of agency and culpability than most critiques of Miller have allowed for. The dialectical materialism of leftist thinkers like Abram Leon is well suited to address this gap. Even when the critique of certain instances of antisemitism makes sense, firing every single person who ever spoke favourably about Miller, signed a letter in support of him, or decided to fund Miller's and his colleagues' research cannot be a solution. Being implicated in antisemitism is not a sufficient reason to have one's fundamental rights violated. Assuming reasonable and well-informed critics of antisemitism would not support taking drastic action against all people who may be complicit in reservoir-style antisemitism, then what relevant distinction might legitimate a different approach to Miller in particular?

The borderlines between the problematically antisemitic and the unacceptably antisemitic are intrinsically subjective. The existence of a fluid border does not mean that antisemitism cannot be challenged; it simply means that we should be wary of what institutions and which individuals we empower to draw such distinctions, and of the consequences that follow from them. We should recognize that the way in which these distinctions are drawn in any given context often has a great deal more to do with the political alliances of those empowered to judge than with the presence or absence of antisemitism. While the critique of antisemitism is a permanent imperative, it is impossible to fully or satisfactorily abstract this mandate from the critique of other cultural and social prejudices. Hate-crime legislation and laws against harassment exist in order to adjudicate situations in which antisemitic sentiment reaches beyond speech and becomes action. In the realm of ideas, however, the distinction between the problematically antisemitic, which can be resolved through education and debate, and the unacceptably antisemitic, at which point the guilty parties must be dismissed from their positions and otherwise silenced, is impossible to make in legally valid terms within a democratic society.

The reservoir theory of antisemitism provides a useful set of tools for discerning the ubiquity of antisemitism in our everyday lives – particularly when it is complemented with a dialectical-materialist approach that takes account of wider social and political issues. But we endanger ourselves when we entrust the state (or state-funded institutions, including universities) to engage equally with varieties of antisemitism, which should be discredited through argument, and the unacceptably antisemitic, which merits punishment (such as termination of employment). States and other public institutions that routinely collapse this distinction are often more invested in accumulating power than administering justice. Their judgements are driven less by a pursuit of accuracy and accountability than by political expediency.

I see no prospect for this situation to change under current political conditions, until we adopt a wider understanding of and appreciation for free speech that would bring it into alignment with the struggle against antisemitism and enhance our commitment to Palestinian freedom. This means rejecting all group-specific definitions of racism, whether that of the IHRA, the JDA, or the many definitions of Islamophobia in circulation.[63] The most effective way of combating racism is by eliminating – through the force of law as well as through education – institutional discrimination. Group-specific definitions of racism by contrast are weak instruments for administering justice.

While the state must suppress and punish violent acts driven by racist intent, reservoir-style racism in individuals is most effectively combated outside the coercive apparatus of the state. The measures taken by the state and non-governmental entities to reduce reservoir-style racism ought to focus on expanding the horizons of those who unwittingly propagate prejudice, rather than on punishment and suppression. To insist that the state should focus on preventing antisemitic violence and institutional discrimination is not to argue that there is nothing we can do to resist cultural or reservoir-style antisemitism. It is simply to recognize that the agency for fighting the reservoir of antisemitism that is an inherited part of our culture must come from people and institutions that are not likely to compromise for the sake of political gain, as all politicians inevitably are. Education can help to dispel antisemitism, but people must be allowed to decide for themselves and draw their own conclusions if critical thought and democratic deliberation are to be encouraged.

Putting such checks and balances in place precludes firing individuals simply for expressing views that may be complicit in antisemitic conspiracy theories. Anti-racism does not justify the violation of due process. If it is acceptable to fire a professor for the encouragement his work gives to reservoir-style antisemitism or other forms of racism, then when and where will the purges end? Is everyone who ever participated in this most ancient of prejudices to be banished from the commonwealth? It should not be necessary to agree with Miller in order to be disturbed by his termination. A more effective – and more materialist – way of fighting antisemitism is to change the political and sociological conditions that allow racism to flourish.

Epilogue: Who Is a Jew? Personal Reflections on Jewish Questions

I am not a specialist in Jewish studies, let alone in the study of antisemitism. Nor, according to most conventional definitions, am I a Jew. What led me to write a book that follows in a tradition pioneered by Karl Marx, Leon Trotsky, Abram Leon, and Isaac Deutscher? What qualifies me to comment on this matter, as if the fate of being Jewish could be chosen and discarded at will? Just who do I think I am? What right do I have to speak at all? I am merely someone who was accused, at a significant juncture in her life, of being an antisemite, and whose personal and professional life was transformed by that accusation. Paradoxically, this accusation put pressure on me to clarify my relationship to the Jewish traditions that have formed me intellectually, as well as to the Jewish histories that occupy the margins of my family history and shaped the fates of ancestors I never knew.

For most of my childhood, my family's Jewish origins were an open secret. At best, they were a source of exotic anecdotes that no one wanted to reckon with. The antisemitism that underlies this long tradition of suppression had gone unremarked for my entire life. Many of those who knew about my family's suppressed history are no longer alive. I bring this history to light without the benefit of their insights, as if relating the story of someone other than myself.

Even further invalidating my perspective on the Jewish question in the eyes of some, I am an ardent opponent of nation-state formations in general, and of settler-colonialism in Palestine specifically. I lived in Palestine while working in Jerusalem, but after a year of such a life, my complicity with the occupation became untenable – a complicity which much of my subsequent work has been an attempt to reckon with. My connection to the Jewish question is, in the eyes of my accusers, more that of the antisemite than of the Jew. In 2019, the same groups that accused me of antisemitism alleged that I had falsified my Jewish identity by signing a letter addressed to the German parliament in which I added my voice to those of hundreds of Jewish scholars and activists expressing concern over the way in which antisemitism was being used to suppress criticism of Israel.[1] In fact, I had only signed the letter because its authors had asked me to. Whether they considered me Jewish or not, I do not know. But I welcomed the opportunity to identify as a Jew, or with Jews, and to associate myself with the search for a better approach to antisemitism, whether or not advocates of the IHRA definition accepted that ascription.

The accusation that I had falsified my Judaism – although I had merely aligned myself with the signatories who identified as Jews, not intentionally claimed that I *was* Jewish – set me on a path. I wanted to understand what it meant to identify as a Jew in my own sense and on my own terms. Identifying as a Jew – or more precisely, identifying *with* Jews – means having a concept of antisemitism, and concepts of antisemitism are as various as Jewish identity itself. The ways in which we perceive, and do not perceive, antisemitism determine how we perceive, or do not perceive, ourselves as Jews. This in turn shapes what we think should be done about antisemitism and its persistence in our social worlds.

In the nineteenth century, the Jewish Question referred to the emancipation of Jews within modern Europe. In the second half of the twentieth century, the Jewish Question meant – in practice if not in theory – Jews' relationship to the state of Israel and the occupation of Palestine. In the twenty-first century, this third iteration of the Jewish Question has been dominated by definitions of antisemitism and debates around how they impinge on the struggle for Palestinian freedom. My reflections on the twenty-first century Jewish Question begin with intertwined narratives of Jews from across Eastern Europe that shaped my family's history, but were subsequently suppressed. If there is one thing I have learned through my study of antisemitism past and present, it is that personal experience overwhelmingly shapes Jewish identity, generating its irreconcilable contradictions and predetermining the political alliances forged in the struggle against antisemitism.

I never thought seriously about my family's suppressed Jewish histories until I was accused of antisemitism. Like many people of European origin, my ancestry begins in the shtetls of Poland and the Jewish settlements of southern Germany, among Jews who were forced, for their economic as well as physical survival, to migrate across the world in search of peace and prosperity. The Jewish link is on both sides of my father's family: his grandmother was descended from a line of wealthy western European Jews who settled in England, Germany, the Netherlands, and ultimately the United States. They belonged to an eminent merchant diaspora and established themselves elegantly wherever they went. Eighteenth- and nineteenth-century England was full of Jews who bore the name Levy. My great-great-grandfather John Jonah Levy was among them.

John Jonah Levy was the son of Joseph Levy, who emigrated with his seven children and wife to the United States, where he died in 1908. By the beginning of the nineteenth century, the Levy family had already made it to the United States. Prior to that, the family can be found in Amsterdam among a long lineage of captains who made a living, and perhaps a fortune, trading goods between the New World of America and the Old World. These ancestors blended well into European society. Their names – Captain Hendrikus Arnoldus Blankman, Captain Gerrit Gerritsz, and Gerrit Pieterszoon Blankman – are not markedly Jewish. One wonders how public these captains were about their ancestry. The Levy name creeps up every other generation within this family line, as if every generation that was determined to suppress its Jewish heritage was followed by another that was equally determined to celebrate it.

Ironically, it was the poor side of my grandfather's family that came from the shtetls of Poland, not the wealthier branch that came from western Europe, that created wealth for generations to come. My grandfather's father, Leon Goldstone, came from much humbler Jewish origins than did his grandmother. Leon was the son of Jacob Goldstein. The wealth that these Jewish migrants created made my father and his seven siblings the beneficiaries of an inheritance that ended with his generation.

Born in an unidentified part of Poland (extant documents are opaque), Jacob Goldstein changed his name to Goldstone, probably when he arrived in America. Having changed from Goldstein to Goldstone, by the next generation it had already become Gould, the Jewish origins of the name entirely obliterated. Herein lies a partial mystery. Newspapers from the time report that Jacob Goldstone was a proud Jew, and his wife was descended from a family of Orthodox Polish rabbis. The evidence of concealed Jewish origins is impossible to deny. The profile of Jacob Goldstone in the *San Francisco Examiner* as the oldest member of the Congregation Sherith Israel in San Francisco's oldest synagogue is not suggestive of someone who would easily renounce his faith or change his name in order to hide his Jewish origins. And yet Jacob was also a talented and committed businessman; he was keenly interested in establishing himself in American commerce. Presumably he made the choices he made – such as concealing certain parts of his history and identity – because he thought doing so was a necessary condition for financial success and upward economic mobility.

Soon after arriving in America, Jacob founded Goldstone Manufacturers, a firm that specialized in pants, overalls, and the crucial element of workers' uniforms that would later be called blue jeans. The family business flourished throughout the late nineteenth century and into the early twentieth century, when Jacob's sons took charge of what then became Goldstone Brothers Manufacturers. Credit for introducing blue jeans into the American economy would go to another entrepreneur, Levi Strauss, a German manufacturer of Ashkenazi Jewish origin who migrated to America around the same time as my great-great-grandfather Jacob, and started his own manufacturing company. Both firms clothed the miners of California's Gold Rush during the 1840s and 1850s. Ultimately, the profits and success of Levi Jeans would entirely eclipse the revenues generated by Goldstone Manufacturers. No one has heard of Goldstone's overalls today. But in its heyday the company was among the leading clothing manufacturers in the western United States.

A 1920 issue of the *San Francisco Examiner* advertised the Goldstone Brothers' slogan, 'Union Made Overalls – Pants Working Clothing', alongside an announcement stating that they were among 'the Progressive Firms Who Are Backing the Movement to Make San Francisco the Wholesale Center of the Pacific Coast'. In 1925, Jacob Goldstone was remembered in his obituary in the *San Francisco Examiner* as 'a pioneer clothing manufacturer of San Francisco'. The label 'pioneer' resonated in more ways than one: the Goldstone family settled permanently, like the Levys, on the West Coast while the Gold Rush was in full swing. They were proud, ambitious, and soon-to-be-wealthy pioneers, unlike the Jews of the tenements, whose stories and demographics dominate early-twentieth-century American history. And yet, behind the Goldstones' story of success and economic prosperity lies a longer history of persecution and poverty, which my father's ancestors share in common with most Jews from the Pale of Settlement – the ancestors of Luxemburg, Leon, Deutscher, and other Polish Jews clustered into communities called shtetls.

There is a break in the family history between Jacob Goldstone, born in an unnamed village in Poland, and his father

Moses David Cohn, born in 1817 in Klepno, Poland, to Rabbi Salomon Kohn. When he was buried in 1887 in San Francisco, Moses' tombstone recorded that he had Germanized his name as Kempen, and described him as 'a native of Kempen, Prussia'. Jacob Goldstein, born in 1832, was Moses' first son.

By the time of my father's birth, the family's Jewish histories had been thoroughly suppressed. I do not know exactly what my father knew about his ancestors' Jewish past because he rarely spoke about it; my own reconstructions are based more on newspaper clippings and genealogical records than on the words of anyone I personally knew. All that I recall being told as a child was that Mabel Levy Goldstone, my father's grandmother and the descendent of the wealthy German Jewish strand of our family, vowed in her will that anyone among her descendants who rejected the Jewish faith and converted to Catholicism would be barred from inheriting her wealth.

Prohibitions notwithstanding, my grandfather did convert to Catholicism when he married my father's mother, and his conversion did not prevent him from inheriting the family's wealth. My father grew up in a conservative Catholic household in which the faith of his Irish mother dominated over that of his Jewish Polish father. I never met his father, and only knew his mother from a distance. The family was wealthy, far above the social class into which I was born and raised. Hence, I never thought of my family as Jewish in even the remotest sense of the term. Had I been pressed, I would have described my father's family as Catholic, born to wealth and entitlement, and oblivious with respect to their own past.

What does my family's history and my efforts to recover it have to do with the study of antisemitism in relationship to Israel/ Palestine, or with the persistence of the Jewish question in the twenty-first century? By demonstrating the ubiquity of anti-semitism in modern society, this history confirms Feldman's account of antisemitism as a reservoir that is 'replenished over time', with every new generation and every new prejudice.[2] Yet, most of those who replenish the reservoir of antisemitism do not see themselves as antisemites.

Feldman's understanding of antisemitism as an everyday phenomenon has illuminated my efforts to trace my own complicity and entanglement with this form of prejudice. It has also helped me to see how my family's history is in part a result of a deep cultural legacy of Jew-hatred, among many other factors. Most importantly, it has awakened me to the antisemitic sentiments that underwrite the most banal and routine social interactions within my everyday social milieu, including in my interactions with anti-racist leftists. I will limit myself to just one example, which I choose because I would not have perceived the antisemitic dimensions of this incident prior to being accused of antisemitism myself and embarking on a journey of self-exploration, which included learning from Feldman's work.

In the summer of 2018, I was invited to a dinner party with a group of fellow academics at a university I was visiting in the north-eastern United States. After dinner, the conversation turned to gossip about university administrators and the politics of our professions. Many of us had attended a public discussion earlier that day of Jasbir Puar's *The Right to Maim: Debility, Capacity, Disability* (2017), a book on the Israeli assault on Gaza and its maiming of Palestinians. A newly hired assistant professor of history had joined the discussion. While we spoke about Palestinians who had been maimed by IDF bombings and attacks, she referred to her time in Israel, during which she had interviewed Israeli veterans maimed by war. At the time when she made the remark, nothing struck me as unusual about her reference to Israeli victims of war. But now, at dinner, as we rehearsed the key points of that discussion, the host's animus came to the fore. Now among like-minded leftists who could be presumed to be hostile to Israel, she felt free to speak her mind.

'What did you think of that Little Miss Zionist?' the host asked. The reduction of the new colleague's comments about

Israel to mere propaganda for the Zionist side was a slight surprise, but the transformation of this person into 'Little Miss Zionist' was the real shock. I had interpreted the new colleague's comments as a reasonable attempt to add historical context to the conversation by reporting her experience of the war on the Israeli side and drawing on her own research. Everyone suffers from war, even when the balance of suffering is unequal, and even when one side bears the blame much more than the other. While I could easily see why we might want to turn away from the perpetrators in order to focus on the real victims of the war in Gaza, the shift to 'Zionism' as the primary discursive space seemed to come from a different kind of reservoir, one full of animosity towards Jews, or at least Israelis.

Zionism was not under discussion during that meeting, yet my leftist friend turned the event into a referendum on that very subject – and, even worse, an attempt to vindicate a Zionist position. Clearly, her remarks did not engage with this new colleague's actual words. Zionism was projected onto her by her antagonist. The new colleague had never said a word about Zionism, or indeed about Israeli politics. Indeed, this new colleague's Jewish name apparently predisposed her to being perceived as a Zionist shill in the eyes of my colleague, even before she opened her mouth.

As I reflected on the after-dinner conversation on my way home, the antisemitic undertone of an exchange I would not have regarded as problematic years earlier came into focus. I came to see how antisemitism can masquerade as anti-Zionism, or as devotion to the Palestinian cause. What I had witnessed was 'reservoir style' antisemitism, to use Feldman's metaphor, at work. During my time in the West Bank, I had repeatedly witnessed overt racism towards Palestinians in Israel, of a much more explicit nature than what I encountered at the New England dinner table.

When I was living in Bethlehem, I met a taxi driver at Checkpoint 300 who offered to take me to what he promised was an important historical site. It turned out to be Herodion (Jabal al-Firdous – 'Mountain of Paradise'), a cone-shaped hill located between the Palestinian villages of Za'atara and Jannatah. It was here that, over two thousand years ago, King Herod built a site to commemorate his life and work. The site was conquered by Romans in the year 71 CE. Many centuries later, the Crusaders fought Salah al-Din when he reclaimed Jerusalem, or so the story goes. More recently, in 1993, Herodium was incorporated into Area C of the Oslo Accords, placed under the control of the Israeli Civil Administration, and managed by the Israel Nature and Parks Authority. Although located in the West Bank, the site is staffed entirely by Israelis. Entry to the site was blocked by a makeshift kiosk. The ticket seller inside refused point blank to allow entry to my Palestinian driver. 'Palestinians not allowed', he said simply. The driver backed away, and I was filled with shame.

This moment returns to me whenever Israeli apartheid is mentioned: never in my life had I witnessed a more direct expression of racism. The manifestation of antisemitism that I observed in this small New England university community was more subtle. In this respect, it was not unlike the WASP antisemitism of the United States during the 1950s, full of upper-class elitism and self-righteousness, which animates the fictions of writers like John Cheever. (My anti-racist colleagues who discoursed against Zionism would of course be horrified by this comparison.) For those like me who are not accustomed to perceiving racism in this sublimated form, its discernment requires a special kind of training and experience. I had to unlearn the cultural norms I had taken for granted for much of my life.

It seemed clear to me that the host herself had a kind of false consciousness about her own attitudes; she had no antisemitic intent, and presumably no conscious hostility to Jews as Jews. Yet the labelling of this new colleague as 'Little Miss Zionist' was nonetheless antisemitic in its unwarranted reduction of a human being to a political symbol. The new colleague was unfairly reduced to a political discourse that she did not deliberately evoke or openly embrace. Like any other racism, antisemitism can exist in the absence of intent. Like Islamophobia, it can simply involve the automatic and evidence-free ascription of a specific ideology to another person. I would not have perceived this reductive discourse as antisemitic a year earlier, yet it seemed obvious to me now, even though my opposition to Zionism was the same as before and my support for Palestinian rights had not changed. As I mulled over the epithet on my way home, a shockwave travelled through me. Although I was troubled by the quick rush to judgement, I did not say anything. It was hard for me to face the fact that this new friend whose company I enjoyed and whose intellect I respected was comfortable airing uncritical antisemitic prejudices. Rightly or wrongly, I kept my silence.

I dwell on this incident because I would not have been disturbed by this offhand description of a political antagonist as 'Little Miss Zionist' prior to being accused of antisemitism myself. That accusation motivated me to seek to understand why and how a purely political remark might be experienced as antisemitic. Being accused of antisemitism awakened me to the prevalence and extent of antisemitism in my own midst. It showed me that my own culture – including the leftist circles of which I was a part – was steeped in antisemitism, not in the sense of outright animus, but in the sense of Feldman's cultural reservoir. From time to time, this reservoir bursts and water overflows. Most of the time, the water flows calmly onwards. Sometimes, the reservoir is just a stagnant pool of tepid water. Without foolishly trying to predict what the future holds, we know that historical wounds inflicted by millennia of persecution will not simply heal and be forgotten. No definition can replace the difficult work of self-recognition that challenging racism and antisemitism in all its forms requires.

The materials left behind in archives, newspapers, and the stories passed from generation to generation suggest that my ancestors participated in the antisemitic reservoirs of German, Polish, Australian, and American society, while also being their target. The shame of being Jewish, and his indifference to the faith of his ancestors, prompted my grandfather to change the family name from Goldstone to Gould – inadvertently echoing the earlier transformation of Goldstein into Goldstone – and to raise his eight children as Catholic. The Jewish traditions that my best-known Jewish ancestor, Rabbi Meschullam Salomon Kohn of Krotoszyn, Rawicz, and Fürth, passed on to his children, which those children passed onto their children, ended with my grandfather Richard Stanley Gould, who died many years before I was born. Although Richard had been raised in a Jewish household, he chose to raise his children in the Catholic faith. The secure social status that came with passing as Catholic prevailed over the shame of being a Jew.

Having chronicled the fates of my obscure ancestors, I will end by contrasting them with those of the much more famous Polish and Russian Jews who have shaped my understanding of antisemitism. These individuals have a tremendous contribution to make to the contemporary effort to bring the fight against antisemitism into alignment with Palestinian freedom. Leon Abram and Isaac Deutscher are among the most outstanding figures in the Jewish-Marxist tradition that insists on the necessary interdependency of Jewish and Palestinian rights – but they are not the only ones. Like Jacob Goldstone, these Jews grew up in the shtetls of Poland, amid intense poverty. As 'non-Jewish Jews' in Deutscher's sense, they used their exposure to the rigorous traditions of Jewish learning to develop philosophies that prioritized human equality and collective freedom above all else, including religion. They applied their learning mainly to non-Jewish domains of learning and political activism, most notably Marxism and Zionism. By contrast, among my ancestors, the tradition of Jewish learning seems to have ended with Rabbi Meschullam Salomon Kohn, towards the beginning of the nineteenth century. Rabbi Kohn died in the southern German city of Fürth, known as 'Franconian Jerusalem' because of its large Jewish population prior to World War II. He was buried in one of Germany's largest Jewish cemeteries, and his tombstone remains untarnished to this day, even after the desecration of Jewish gravestones by the Nazis. The traces left by these ancestors are scarce. As a Polish archivist remarked to me, 'The obligation to keep Jewish vital records in this area was first introduced in 1794.'[3] Whatever records did exist have not made it to the present.

Aside from Rabbi Meschullam Salomon Kohn, my ancestors were traders, merchants, and businessmen, not scholars keeping the Jewish faith alive. Their pragmatism may have contributed to their willingness to convert to Catholicism when success seemed to demand this sacrifice. Their relative indifference to the faith of their ancestors, which increased with every generation, meant that I was not raised in the Jewish tradition. Until I was accused of being an antisemite, I had no consciousness of being affected by antisemitism. Antisemitism had little meaning for me personally, either as a prejudice of which I was a victim or as a phenomenon in which I was implicated. It was at this juncture in my life that David Feldman's argument about antisemitism as a reservoir that is 'replenished over time', and which we all inherit to a greater or lesser degree, acquired a special kind of meaning for me.

During my journey through the history of antisemitism and the debate around its definitions, I have encountered only one voice in the debate about the IHRA definition and the wider controversy around defining antisemitism that is consistently and uncompromisingly devoted to free speech, without caveats or self-deceptions. It belongs to Ken Stern, author of the important account of the campus politics pertaining to this definition, *The Conflict over the Conflict* (2020). Stern is unique in that he has never, in any way known to me, misrepresented the positions of his opponents due to political blindness. Nor has he sought to deflect good-faith debates around free speech and anti-semitism in directions more suited to his political agenda. Even scholars of free speech who have written about antisemitism have not maintained his high standards. Ever since acquiring a reputation in leftist circles for his opposition to the abusive application of the IHRA definition, which he authored, Stern has displayed a capacity for self-critique and objective judgement in this debate that strengthens the free-speech argument more broadly.[4] If all participants in this debate had his intellectual honesty, there might be no conflict at all, or at least people would be honest about their disagreement. However, in this case, virtue is the fatal flaw. Stern's approach cannot be generally applied because he is the only participant in the debate whose track record suggests a serious concern for free speech – and it is impossible to build a lasting paradigm for free speech around a single individual.

Who among us is ready to grant the right of our political antagonists to disagree and yet continue to exist, in opposition to us? I have seen leading scholars of free speech engage in self-deception time and again, whether by disproportionately favouring causes that suit their political disposition, or by implicitly supporting the censorship of views they oppose.[5] I have no reason to consider myself exempt from such self-deception. At the risk of self-incrimination, I will suggest that part of the problem with academic work on free speech is that the authors in question are all university-based academics, and the very structure of academic life encourages a strong bifurcation between theory and practice. Academics are rarely if ever forced to confront the actual contexts in which their ideas are implemented. When they do confront contemporary contexts, it is by choice rather than necessity, and therefore they do so selectively. This severance from practice means that the sophisticated body of academic scholarship that has developed around free speech in the past several decades is often out of touch with the everyday scenarios in which free speech is undermined and contested, and its proponents are rarely called on to confront the contradictions in their arguments or commitments. Their theoretical defences of free speech thus end up existing independently of the world in which they should be implemented.

I have searched throughout this book for ways of fighting antisemitism while also preventing this necessary fight from suppressing and constraining pro-Palestinian activism. I have not been so naive as to believe that I could develop a straightforward path for eradicating antisemitism that has any hope of achieving a consensus in the current polarized environment. And yet I do believe that the materialist critique of antisemitism developed in the preceding century by Leon, Trotsky, and Deutscher can be of use today in showing how the struggle for Palestinian freedom and the fight against antisemitism demand each other. If 'unconditional solidarity with the persecuted and exterminated' is what made Isaac Deutscher a Jew in his own estimation, then fidelity to Judaism mandates a future for Jews that incorporates into itself the quest for Palestinian freedom.

Appreciation

Tremendous thanks to Kayvan Tahmasebian for being the first reader of this book, and for accompanying me on my journey away from purely academic writing to addressing a wider audience. My mother Brenda Gould was immensely generous with her time and careful reading. Kate and Beth Gould helped with framing the book in a wider context.

I am very grateful to the Society of Authors for awarding this book a work in progress grant at an early stage. At Verso, I am indebted to Rosie Warren for her wonderful edits, Charles Peyton for brilliant copyediting, Jeanne Tao for overseeing the production process, and Tariq Ali and Sebastian Budgen for inviting me to write the book. I also want to express my gratitude to Lynn Wadding, who went out of her way to make it possible for me to attend all screenings of the Bristol Palestine Film Festival in 2021. Her extraordinary care and concern have been inspiring in their own right. Thanks to Tariq Modood, Tom Sperlinger, Gene Feder, the members of the British Committee for the Universities of Palestine, and their solidarity with me from 2017, when I first became entangled in these issues while at the University of Bristol. Thanks to Eric Heinze, whose work on academic freedom and freedom of speech has long been an inspiration to me. Other scholars, friends, and colleagues to whom I owe significant debts include Seth Anziska, Sue Blackwell, Mona Baker, Mohammad El-Khatib, Kate Gould, Talal Hangari, Bilal Hamamra, Javed Majeed, Malaka Mohammad Shwaikh, Riz Mokal, Yossi Rappaport, Yana Shabana, Jonathan Rosenhead,

Kenneth Stern, Marc Volovici, and Yair Wallach. Jamie Potter at the law firm Bindmans LLP was an extraordinary lawyer and source of inspiration. His example provided a much-needed reminder that the law can be used to advance social justice. In expressing my gratitude to these individuals, which in some cases is due to their honest and eye-opening disagreements with me, I do not of course imply any agreement on their part with my views.

This book is dedicated to the memory of my father, Christopher Joseph Gould, who passed away unexpectedly before it was completed. I wish he could have lived to see it. I am grateful to be able to honour his lifelong commitment to freedom of speech.

Notes

Prologue: On Being Accused of Antisemitism

1. I have described this bifurcated existence in Rebecca Ruth Gould, 'The Materiality of Resistance: Israel's Apartheid Wall in an Age of Globalization', *Social Text* 118 (2014), pp. 1–22.
2. Edward Said, *Out of Place: A Memoir* (New York: Vintage, 1999), p. 134.
3. The online version of this document identifies the Van Leer Institute as the place where 'a group of scholars . . . came together . . . to address key challenges in identifying and confronting antisemitism' (jerusalemdeclaration.org).
4. Rebecca Ruth Gould, 'Stolen Limestone', *Beautiful English* (Scotland: Dreich), p. 22.
5. The stories behind these limestone deposits are told in Andrew Ross, *Stone Men: The Palestinians Who Built Israel* (London: Verso, 2019).
6. The article was published as Rebecca Gould, 'Beyond Anti-Semitism', *Counterpunch* 18: 19, pp. 1–3. This was before *Counterpunch* was an exclusively online publication.
7. Isaac Deutscher, 'Interview with Isaac Deutscher: On the Israeli–Arab War', *New Left Review* I/44 (July–August 1967), p. 43.
8. Gould, 'Beyond Anti-Semitism', p. 3.
9. By contrast, *The Holocaust and the Nakba: A New Grammar of Trauma and History*, ed. Bashir Bashir and Amos Goldberg (New York: Columbia University Press, 2018), develops a nuanced methodology for placing Palestinian and Jewish trauma in comparison.
10. Camilla Turner, 'Bristol University Investigates Claims of Anti-Semitism after Lecturer Claims that Jews Should Stop "Privileging" the Holocaust', *Daily Telegraph*, 20 February 2017.
11. Letter from Marie Van der Zyl, vice-president of the Board of Deputies of British Jews, to Vice Chancellor Hugh Brady, 22 February 2017, on file with the author.

12. Cited in Paul Mendes-Flohr and Jehuda Reinharz, eds, *The Jew in the Modern World: A Documentary History* (Oxford: Oxford University Press, 1995), p. 580.

13. For background on the conflict around the IHRA definition within the Labour Party, see Jamie Stern-Weiner, ed., *Antisemitism and the Labour Party* (London: Verso, 2019). The text for the IHRA definition is posted on the website of the International Holocaust Remembrance Alliance, at holocaustremembrance.com. My quotations from the definition refer to this source.

14. Brian Klug, 'Interrogating "New Anti-Semitism"', *Ethnic and Racial Studies* 36: 3 (2013), p. 470.

15. Office to Monitor and Combat Anti-Semitism, '"Working Definition" of Anti-Semitism', 8 February 2007, at 2001-2009.state.gov.

16. Kenneth S. Stern, *The Conflict over the Conflict: The Israel/Palestine Campus Debate* (Toronto: New Jewish Press, 2020), p. 151.

17. Kenneth S. Stern, *Antisemitism Today: How It Is the Same, How It Is Different, and How to Fight It* (American Jewish Committee, 2006), p. 192.

18. *Antisemitism in 2016: Overview, Trends and Events* (Jerusalem: Ministry of Diaspora Affairs, 2017), p. 52.

19. Stern, *Antisemitism Today*, p. 102. My emphases.

20. Rabbi Andrew Baker, Deidre Berger, and Michael Whine, MBE, 'Letter to Kathrin Meyer and Katharina von Schnurbein', 19 January 2021, ecaj.org.au/wordpress/wp-content/uploads/Baker-Berger -Whine-Letter-on-Origins-of-the-WD.pdf. Baker, Berger, and Whine identify themselves, along with Stern, as joint authors of the original definition in 2004–05.

21. The history of these events in documented in Stern, *Conflict over the Conflict*.

22. Dina Porat and Esther Webman, *Compilation Booklet of the Proceedings of 'The Working Definition of Antisemitism – Six Years After'* (Tel Aviv: The Stephen Roth Institute for the Study of Contemporary Antisemitism and Racism, Tel Aviv University, 2010), p. 4.

23. Antony Lerman, 'Weapons in the Labour Antisemitism Wars? The IHRA Working Definition and the Accusation of "Institutional Antisemitism"', in Greg Philo et al., *Bad News for Labour: Antisemitism, the Party and Public Belief* (London: Pluto, 2019), p. 122; Jamie Stern-Weiner, 'The Politics of a Definition: How the IHRA Working Definition of Antisemitism Is Being Misrepresented', *Free Speech on Israel*, April 2021, pp. 14ff. PDF available at free speechonisrael.org.uk.

24. Ben White, 'Discredited Definition of Anti-Semitism No Longer in Use, Says BBC', *Electronic Intifada*, 30 October 2013.

25. 'SWC Contributes to New EU Handbook for the Practical Use of the IHRA "Working Definition of Antisemitism"', 8 January 2021, *Simon Wiesenthal Center*, wiesenthal.com.

26. See Stern-Weiner, 'Politics of a Definition'.

27. The Pears Foundation later withdrew its name from the Center, apparently due to the stance Feldman had taken against the IHRA definition.

28. David Feldman, 'Will Britain's New Definition of Antisemitism Help Jewish People? I'm Sceptical', *Guardian*, 28 December 2016.

29. Detailed accounts of the process through which this association took place are offered in Stern-Weiner, 'Politics of a Definition', and Anthony Lerman, *Whatever Happened to Antisemitism? Redefinition and the Myth of the 'Collective Jew'* (London: Pluto, 2022).

30. All quotations are from this report, entitled 'Report to the Deputy Vice-Chancellor' (17 April 2017), on file with the author.

31. 'Anti-Semitism Expert and UK Government Advisor Clash over IHRA Definition', *Middle East Monitor*, 30 December 2020.

32. Jo Johnson, 'Tackling Anti-Semitism on Campus', 13 February 2017. In the University of Bristol's report (on file with the author) the letter is incorrectly dated as being from 2016.

33. Gavin Williamson, 'International Holocaust Remembrance Alliance (IHRA) Working Definition of Antisemitism', 9 October 2020.

34. 'Guidance to the Office for Students (OfS) – Secretary of State's Strategic Priorities', 8 February 2021, p. 7.

35. 'Providers that Have Adopted the IHRA Working Definition of Antisemitism', *Office for Students*, officeforstudents.org.uk/media/5920824e-b9e9-44ba-aec5-8aec0d6000b6/providers-that-have-adopted-the-ihra-working-definition-of-antisemitism_05-07-2022.pdf (last updated 5 July 2022).

36. Smita Jamdar, 'Gavin Williamson's Letter to Vice Chancellors on the IHRA Definition of Antisemitism', Shakespeare Martineau blog, 13 October 2020, shma.co.uk.

37. Shahd Abusalama, interviewed on *Not the Andrew Marr Show*, 10 January 2023, starting at 2 minutes.

38. Karl Marx, '*Letters from the Deutsch-Französische Jahrbücher*: Marx to Ruge, Kreuznach, September 1843', at marxists.org.

1. Erasing Palestine

1. On this process as reflected in the Israeli media, see Yana Shabana, 'Terrorism Frames and Indigenous Elimination in News Translation: The *Times of Israel* as a Case Study', PhD dissertation, University of Birmingham, 2022.

2. This link was first pursued in the pioneering work of Nadia Abou El-Haj, *Facts on the Ground: Archaeological Practice and Territorial Self-Fashioning in Israeli Society* (Chicago: University of Chicago Press, 2001).

3. 'Jerusalem Embassy Act of 1995', 104th US Congress, 1st Session, S. 1322.

4. Mick Dumper, 'The US Embassy Move to Jerusalem: Mixed Messages and Mixed Blessings for Israel?' *Review of Middle East Studies* 53: 1 (2019), p. 37.

5. The President of the United States of America, 'Recognizing Jerusalem as the Capital of the State of Israel and Relocating the United States Embassy to Israel to Jerusalem', *Federal Register* 82: 236 (11 December 2017).

6. The history of the wall and the art that has been created on it is discussed in Gerhard Wolf and Avinoam Shalem, *Facing the Wall: The Palestinian-Israeli Barriers* (Köln: König, 2011), and Rebecca Ruth Gould, 'The Materiality of Resistance: Israel's Apartheid Wall in an Age of Globalization', *Social Text* 118 (March 2014).

7. Eyal Weizman, *Hollow Land: Israel's Architecture of Occupation* (New York: Verso, 2007), p. 149.

8. United Nations Office for the Coordination of Humanitarian Affairs, 'Over 700 Road Obstacles Control Palestinian Movement within the West Bank', 8 October 2018, at ochaopt.org.

9. Hagar Kotef and Merav Amir, 'Between Imaginary Lines: Violence and Its Justifications at the Military Checkpoints in Occupied Palestine', *Theory, Culture & Society* 28: 1 (2011), p. 73.

10. Alexandra Rijke and Claudio Minca, 'Inside Checkpoint 300: Checkpoint Regimes as Spatial Political Technologies in the Occupied Palestinian Territories', *Antipode* 51: 3 (2019), p. 968.

11. Nigel Parsons and Mark Salter, 'Israeli Biopolitics: Closure, Territorialisation and Governmentality', *Geopolitics* 13: 4 (2008), p. 709.

12. Michel Foucault, *The History of Sexuality: Volume 1, An Introduction*, transl. Robert Hurley (New York: Vintage, 1976), p. 138.

13. Nirit Anderman, '"Why Should We Ask Israel Permission to Film Its Illegal Activity?"', *Haaretz*, 12 May 2021.

14. I saw both of these films at Bristol's Palestine Film Festival in 2021.

15. By contrast, in some terminals Israeli soldiers use Arabic. Kotef and Amir, 'Between Imaginary Lines', p. 59.

16. 'Palestinian Worker Suffocates While Waiting at Crowded Israeli Military Checkpoint', *Palestine Chronicle* blog post, 7 March 2018.

17. Parsons and Salter, 'Israeli Biopolitics', p. 710.

18. Helga Tawil-Souri, 'New Palestinian Centers: An Ethnography of the "Checkpoint Economy"', *Journal of Cultural Studies* 12 (2009), p. 232.

19. Amira Hass, 'Israel's Closure Policy: An Ineffective Strategy of Containment and Repression', *Journal of Palestine Studies* 31: 3 (2002), p. 6.
20. Kotef and Amir, 'Between Imaginary Lines', p. 73.
21. Hass, 'Israel's Closure Policy', p. 10.
22. Ghassan Kanafani, *Men in the Sun and Other Palestinian Stories*, transl. Hilary Kilpatrick (Boulder, CO: Lynne Rienner, 1999), p. 63.

2. Anti-Zionism before Israel

1. Isaac Deutscher, *The Non-Jewish Jew* (London: Verso, 2017 [1968]), p. 48.
2. Isaac Deutscher, *The Reporter* (27 April and 11 May 1954), marxists.org.
3. Isaac Deutscher, 'Interview with Isaac Deutscher: On the Israeli–Arab War', *New Left Review* I/44 (July–August 1967), p. 36
4. Deutscher, *Non-Jewish Jew*, p. 107.
5. Deutscher, *Non-Jewish Jew*, p. 126.
6. See Didier Musiedlak, 'Wilhelm Marr (1819–1904) and the Left in Germany: The Birth of Modern Antisemitism', in *The European Left and the Jewish Question, 1848–1992*, ed. Allesandra Tarquini (Cham, Switzerland: Palgrave Macmillan, 2021).
7. *Der Arbayter Fraynd*, 9, 15, and 30 June 1916, cited in Stuart Cohen, *English Zionists and British Jews: The Communal Politics of Anglo-Jewry, 1895–1920* (Princeton: Princeton University Press 1982), p. 252.
8. Mark Levene, 'The Balfour Declaration: A Case of Mistaken Identity', *English Historical Review* CVII: CCCCXXII (1992), p. 58.
9. David Lloyd George, *War Memoirs* (London: Weidenfeld & Watson, 1933–36), vol. 2, p. 721.
10. The analysis here is informed by Brian Klug, 'Zionism, Binationalism, Antisemitism: Three Contemporary Jewish Readings of the Balfour Declaration', *Journal of Levantine Studies* 8: 1 (2018).
11. I quote from the manifesto, as reproduced in Nahum Sokolow, *History of Zionism, 1600–1918* (London: Longmans, Green & Co., 1919), pp. 124–8.
12. Jonathan Schneer, *The Balfour Declaration: The Origins of the Arab-Israeli Conflict* (London: Bloomsbury, 2010), p. 307.
13. Levene, 'The Balfour Declaration', p. 63.
14. Levene, 'The Balfour Declaration', p. 67.
15. Schneer, *The Balfour Declaration*, p. 336.
16. Edwin S. Montagu, 'The Anti-Semitism of the Present Government', 23 August 1917, at commons.wikimedia.org.

17. Harry Sacher, *Zionist Portraits* (London: Anthony Blond, 1959), p. 37.
18. C. G. Montefiore, 'An Englishman of Jewish Faith', *Fortnightly Review*, November 1916, p. 823.
19. Levene, 'Balfour Declaration', p. 76.
20. Elizabeth Monroe, *Britain's Moment in the Middle East* (London: Chatto & Windus, 1981), p. 43.
21. Cited in Schneer, *The Balfour Declaration*, p. 343.
22. Cited in Levene, 'The Balfour Declaration', p. 59.
23. As documented in Schneer, *The Balfour Declaration*, pp. 342–4.
24. Levene, 'The Balfour Declaration', p. 75.
25. Levene, 'The Balfour Declaration', p. 77.
26. Quoted in Leon Trotsky, *On the Jewish Question* (New York: Pathfinder, 1970), p. 20.
27. Enzo Traverso, *The Jewish Question: History of a Marxist Debate* (Leiden: Brill, 2018), p. 10. I quote here from the revised second edition of Traverso's classic work, which was first published in 1990.

3. A Materialist Critique of Antisemitism: Introducing Abram Leon

1. See in particular Hannah Arendt, 'Antisemitism', in Arendt, *The Jewish Writings*, ed. Jerome Kohn and Ron H. Feldman (New York: Schocken, 2007), pp. 46–121.
2. The most developed critique is that of Maxime Rodinson, 'From the Jewish Nation to the Jewish Problem', in Rodinson, *Cult, Ghetto, and State: The Persistence of the Jewish Question* (London: Saqi, 1983).
3. Enzo Traverso, *The Jewish Question: History of a Marxist Debate* (Leiden: Brill, 2018), p. 193.
4. David Ruben, 'Marxism and the Jewish Question', *Socialist Register 1982*, p. 210.
5. See John Rose, 'Liberating Jewish History from Its Zionist Stranglehold: Rediscovering Abram Leon', *Holy Land Studies: A Multidisciplinary Journal* 5: 1 (2006), p. 3n3.
6. In this connection it is worth noting that Trotsky's own name was a replacement for the more visibly Jewish Lev Davidovich Bronstein. The most extensive biographical account of Leon is by his friend and fellow activist Ernest Mandel (1923–95), whose memoir of his friendship with Leon appears as the preface to the 1968 French edition, and which is reprinted in Abram Leon, *The Jewish Question: A Marxist Interpretation* (London: Pathfinder, 1970 [1946]).

7. The full print run of the newspaper has been digitized by the Belgian War Press project, at warpress.cegesoma.be.

8. See, for example, Robert Fine and Philip Spencer, 'Marx's Defence of Jewish Emancipation and Critique of the Jewish Question', in Fine and Spencer, *Antisemitism and the Left: On the Return of the Jewish Question* (Manchester: Manchester University Press, 2017).

9. Leon, *The Jewish Question*, p. 77n15.

10. Another example J. A. Hobson, *Imperialism* (London: Allen & Unwin, 1949 [1902]). David Feldman has noted Hobson's antisemitic tendencies in 'Commerce, Capitalism, and Antisemitism', *Jews, Money, Myth*, Jewish Museum London, 2019; and 'Jeremy Corbyn, "Imperialism", and Labour's Antisemitism Problem', *History Workshop Online*, 2019, historyworkshop.org.uk.

11. Leon Trotsky, 'Interview with Jewish Correspondents in Mexico', in Leon Trotsky, *On the Jewish Question* (New York: Pathfinder, 1970), p. 34.

12. In the only article to discuss Leon's contribution to Jewish studies thoroughly, John Rose notes that Leon 'wrote the first pioneering study' of Jewish mercantilism yet 'remains largely unrecognized by modern scholarship' ('Liberating Jewish History', p. 3). Other scholars – for example, Tal Elmaliach in 'The "Revival" of Abram Leon: The "Jewish Question" and the American New Left', *Left History* 21: 2 (2017–18) – have examined Leon's book from more contemporary perspectives, such as its reception after the Six-Day War.

13. Traverso, *The Jewish Question*, p. 10.

14. For Leon's revision of Marx, see Tom Navon, 'Marx and Jewish History', paper delivered at Marx200: Politics – Theory – Socialism, Rosa Luxemburg Stiftung Congress in Berlin, 4 May 2018.

15. Leon Trotsky, 'Imperialism and Anti-semitism', in Trotsky, *On the Jewish Question*, p. 50.

16. Karl Marx, *Capital*, vol. 1, transl. Ben Fowkes (London: Penguin, 1976), p. 173.

17. Marx's dissertation was titled 'Differenz der demokritischen und epikureischen Naturphilosophie' [The difference between the Democritean and Epicurean philosophy of nature], University of Jena, 1841.

18. Bruno Bauer, *Die Judenfrage* (Braunschweig: F. Otto, 1843), p. 9.

19. Traverso, *The Jewish Question*, p. 20.

20. Trotsky, 'Imperialism and Anti-semitism', p. 51.

21. *Oxford English Dictionary*, 'pore, n.1', oed.com, December 2022.

22. Leon, *The Jewish Question*, p. 72.

23. Karl Marx, 'On the Jewish Question', in *Marx: Early Political Writings*, ed. Joseph J. O'Malley (Cambridge: Cambridge University Press, 1994), p. 54.

24. Leon, *The Jewish Question*, p. 79.
25. Leon, *The Jewish Question*, p. 77.
26. Henri Laurent, 'Religion et affaires', *Cahiers du libre examen*, Brussels, 1938, cited in Leon, *The Jewish Question*, p. 77.
27. See Scott Meikle, 'Aristotle on Money', *Phronesis* 39: 1 (1994).
28. David Graeber, *Debt: The First 5,000 Years* (New York: Melville House, 2011).
29. Leon, *The Jewish Question*, p. 154.
30. Max Weber, *Ancient Judaism*, transl. H. H. Girth and Don Martindale (New York: Free Press, 1967 [1917–9]), p. 8. Weber also expands on these ideas in Weber, *The Sociology of Religion*, transl. Ephraim Fischoff (Boston: Beacon, 1963 [1920]).
31. Arnaldo Momigliano, 'A Note on Max Weber's Definition of Judaism as a Pariah-Religion', *History and Theory* 19: 3 (1980).
32. Leon, *The Jewish Question*, p. 91.
33. Leon, *The Jewish Question*, p. 154.
34. Leon, *The Jewish Question*, p. 251.
35. Leon, *The Jewish Question*, p. 252.
36. Leon, *The Jewish Question*, p. 220.
37. Leon, *The Jewish Question*, p. 232.
38. Frantz Fanon, *Black Skin, White Masks* (London: Pluto, 1986), p. 92.
39. Leon, *The Jewish Question*, p. 229.
40. Leon, *The Jewish Question*, p. 244.
41. Leon, *The Jewish Question*, p. 229.
42. Leon, *The Jewish Question*, p. 250.
43. Leon, *The Jewish Question*, p. 205.
44. Leon, *The Jewish Question*, p. 254.
45. Rodinson, 'From the Jewish Nation to the Jewish Problem'.
46. Abram Leon, *Al-Mafhum al-maddi li-l-masalat al-yahudiyya*, transl. Imad Nuwayhid (Beirut: Dar al-Tali'a lil-Taba'a wa al-Nashr, 1969).
47. Nuwayhid's biography is discussed in Dylan Baun, 'Claiming an Individual: Party, Family and the Politics of Memorialization in the Lebanese Civil War', *Middle East Critique* 30: 4 (2021).
48. Tom Navon, 'A Materialist Approach to Jewish History – The Case of Abram Leon', unpublished manuscript, p. 2.
49. Yanis Varoufakis, 'The Global Minotaur: The Crash of 2008 and the Euro-Zone Crisis in Historical Perspective', 9 November 2011, Columbia University, YouTube video, at 55 mins.
50. Leon, *The Jewish Question*, p. 205.
51. Leon, *The Jewish Question*, p. 71.
52. Leon, *The Jewish Question*, p. 72.
53. Leon, *The Jewish Question*, p. 229.

54. Op-eds and letters relying on this argument can be found in venues such as the *Miami Herald* (11 July 2020), the *Guardian* (15 June 2018), and *Jewish News Syndicate* (21 January 2020). Those who disagree on the IHRA definition often agree on this point.

55. Leon, *The Jewish Question*, p. 171.

56. Feldman, 'Jeremy Corbyn, "Imperialism", and Labour's Antisemitism Problem'.

57. David Feldman and Marc Volovici, '"The Pure Essence of Things"? Contingency, Controversy and the Struggle to Define Antisemitism and Islamophobia', in *Antisemitism, Islamophobia, and the Politics of Definition*, ed. David Feldman and Marc Volovici (London: Palgrave, 2023), pp. 3–18.

4. Free Speech and Palestinian Freedom

1. The identity of the QC has not been released or made known to the relevant parties. The university defended its decision to preserve the QC's anonymity as well as the cost of the legal proceedings on the grounds that revealing the amount 'would likely prejudice both the commercial interests of the university and the QC', quoted in Steerpike, 'Bristol Refuse to Declare David Miller Probe Costs', *Spectator*, 6 January 2022.

2. Quoted from 'Bristol – Hate Off Campus: Pattern of Behaviour', UJS – The Voice of Jewish Students website, ujs.org.uk.

3. Personal conversation with David Miller, 4 December 2021.

4. Quoted in Chris York, 'Jewish Students "Intimidated" By Professor's Comments as Williamson Defends "Free Speech"', *Huffington Post*, 20 February 2021.

5. 'PM Speech at Antisemitism Reception', 27 November 2018, gov.uk.

6. See the working paper, co-authored by David Miller, Paul McKeigue, and Piers Robinson, 'Assessment by the Engineering Sub-team of the OPCW Fact-Finding Mission Investigating the Alleged Chemical Attack in Douma in April 2018', *Working Group on Syria, Propaganda and Media*, 13 May 2019. As indicated by the title, this work calls into question the evidence that Syrian president Bashar al-Assad used chemical weapons against a civilian population.

7. Alex Callinicos, 'Defend David Miller and Academic Freedom', *Socialist Worker*, 5 October 2021.

8. Excerpts from the report are shared in *The Electronic Intifada* ('David Miller Was Cleared of Anti-Semitism, Leaked Document Shows', 22 October 2021), which misleadingly fails to clarify that it refers to the complaint of 2019 rather than the incidents of 2021.

9. Victoria Canning (@Vicky_Canning), 'A @ucu member – #David-Miller – has been cleared of unlawful actions and antisemitism. In light of recent developments, @berglund_oscar and I are asking the University', Twitter, 23 October 2021.

10. 'Motion: Academic Freedom and Professor David Miller', *Bristol UCU Notes*, March 2021, bristolucu.files.wordpress.com/2021/03/motion-academic-freedom-and-professor-david-miller.pdf.

11. Eldin Fahmy, via email, 21 October 2021.

12. Talal Hangari, via email, 29 Jan 2022. For the persecution experienced by Hangari, see p. 102.

13. Peter Ramsay offers a critical introduction to this legislation in 'Is Prevent a Safe Space?', *Education, Citizenship and Social Justice* 12: 2 (March 2017).

14. 'University Statement Regarding Complaint against Professor Steven Greer', University of Bristol, 8 October 2021, bristol.ac.uk.

15. Marc Lamont Hill and Mitchell Plitnick, *Except for Palestine: The Limits of Progressive Politics* (New York: New Press, 2020).

16. See Salaita's autobiographical account, *Uncivil Rites: Palestine and the Limits of Academic Freedom* (Chicago: Haymarket, 2015).

17. Syd Waters, 'The Interaction of Academic Freedom and State Sovereignty', in *Normative Tensions: Academic Freedom in International Education*, ed. Kevin W. Gray (Rowman & Littlefield, 2022), pp. 63–4.

18. Malia Bouattia, 'I'm the New NUS President – and No, I'm Not an Antisemitic Isis Sympathiser', *Guardian*, 24 April 2016.

19. These campaigns are detailed in Malaka Shwaikh and Rebecca Ruth Gould, 'The Palestine Exception to Academic Freedom: Intertwined Stories from the Frontlines of UK-Based Palestine Activism', *Biography: An Interdisciplinary Quarterly* 42: 4 (2020).

20. The article that triggered the controversy is Talal Hangari, 'Why We Should Drop the IHRA Definition of Antisemitism', *Cambridge Student*, 7 May 2021. Hangari has documented his experience in 'I Was Expelled from My Labour Club for Disagreeing with the IHRA', *Tribune Magazine*, 9 June 2021.

21. Malia Bouattia, 'What We Should Learn from Shahd Abusalama's Victory against the Hasbara Brigades', *New Arab*, 4 February 2022.

22. 'Solidarity with Shahd Abusalama', Jewish Voice for Labour, 10 January 2023, jewishvoiceforlabour.org.uk.

23. Gareth Harris, 'Manchester Gallery Director Forced Out over Palestine Statement in Exhibition', *Art Newspaper*, 23 February 2022.

24. '100 MPs and Peers Write to Bristol University over Professor David Miller', *Jewish News*, 5 March 2021.

25. 'Educators and Researchers in Support of Professor Miller', Support David Miller, 26 February 2021, supportmiller.org.

26. 'Response to Recent Comments by Prof. David Miller', joint letter, 1 March 2021, wordpress.com.

27. Correspondence on file with author – dated 7 September 2021.

28. Asa Winstanley, 'Professor David Miller Fired after Israel Lobby Smear Campaign', *Electronic Intifada*, 1 October 2021.

29. 'Guide to Freedom of Speech', University of Birmingham, intranet .birmingham.ac.uk.

30. These dynamics are explored in detail in Rebecca Ruth Gould, 'Legal Form and Legal Legitimacy: The IHRA Definition of Anti-semitism as a Case Study in Censored Speech', *Law, Culture and the Humanities* 18: 1 (2018).

31. I explain on pp. 121–5 why the insistence on balance by university free speech codes undermines academic freedom.

32. Equality and Human Rights Commission, *Freedom of Expression: A Guide for Higher Education Providers and Students' Unions in England and Wales*, February 2019, p. 25, equalityhumanrights.com.

33. 'University Statement on PalSoc Event of 8 November 2017', University of Cambridge, 2 February 2018.

34. Sara Ahmed, *Complaint!* (Durham: Duke University Press, 2021).

35. 'University of Aberdeen Votes Against Using IHRA Definition of Anti-Semitism', *National*, 9 October 2022, thenational.scot. The University Senate voted, against the advice of the university administration, to adopt the JDA instead of the IHRA.

36. This essay was published in a shorter version as 'My Life as a Cautionary Tale: Probing the Limits of Academic Freedom', *Chronicle Review*, 28 August 2019. The more substantive version, from which I quote here, is found on the author's website, stevesalaita. com.

37. See Virginia Mantouvalou, '"I Lost My Job Over a Facebook Post – Was That Fair?" Discipline and Dismissal for Social Media Activity', *International Journal of Comparative Labour Law and Industrial Relations* 35: 1 (2019).

38. Isabella B. Cho and Ariel H. Kim, '38 Harvard Faculty Sign Open Letter Questioning Results of Misconduct Investigations into Prof. John Comaroff', *Harvard Crimson*, 4 February 2022. Most of the signatories subsequently retracted their signatures, but, with only a few exceptions, they did not apologize for signing in the first place or shed light on their thought process.

39. Karl Marx, 'On the Jewish Question', in *Marx: Early Political Writings*, ed. Joseph J. O'Malley (Cambridge: Cambridge University Press, 1994), p. 47.

40. Marx, 'On the Jewish Question', p. 50.

41. Karl Marx, 'Comments on the Latest Prussian Censorship Instruction', 1842, at marxists.org. Emphasis in original.

42. Laura Weinrib documents the gradual bifurcation between free speech and leftist politics within the US labour movement in *The Taming of Free Speech: America's Civil Liberties Compromise* (Cambridge, MA: Harvard University Press, 2016).

43. Karl Marx to Arnold Ruge, 30 November 1842, at marxists.org.

44. Together with Columbia University's former provost, Jonathan Cole, Bilgrami also co-edited a major volume on the philosophical foundations for academic freedom in the contemporary academy. See Akeel Bilgrami and Jonathan R. Cole, *Who's Afraid of Academic Freedom?* (New York: Columbia University Press, 2015).

45. Akeel Bilgrami, 'Liberalism and the Academy', in Bilgrami, *Secularism, Identity, and Enchantment* (Cambridge, MA: Harvard University Press, 2014), p. 78.

46. Bilgrami, 'Liberalism and the Academy', 87.

47. David Feldman, 'Commerce, Capitalism, and Antisemitism', in Feldman, *Jews, Money, Myth*, Jewish Museum London, 2019, p. 87.

48. The most detailed account of the reservoir theory of antisemitism is in Ben Gidley, Brendan McGeever, and David Feldman, 'Labour and Antisemitism: A Crisis Misunderstood', *Political Quarterly* 91: 2 (2020). Feldman's authorship is a common denominator in the co-authored works pertaining to the reservoir theory, which makes it possible to associate this theory chiefly with him.

49. See late works such as Arnaldo Momigliano, *Alien Wisdom: The Limits of Hellenization* (Cambridge: Cambridge University Press, 1990).

50. Rebecca Ruth Gould, 'Antiquarianism as Genealogy: Arnaldo Momigliano's Method', *History & Theory* 53: 2 (2014).

51. David Feldman, 'Labour Can Expel Antisemites – But That Won't "Root Out" Antisemitism in Our Culture', *Guardian*, 8 April 2020.

52. This argument is developed further in Rebecca Ruth Gould, 'Is the "Hate" in Hate Speech the "Hate" in Hate Crime? Waldron and Dworkin on Political Legitimacy', *Jurisprudence* 10: 2 (2019).

53. Feldman, 'Labour Can Expel Antisemites'.

54. Bari Weiss, *How to Fight Anti-Semitism* (London: Allen Lane, 2020), p. 146.

55. See David Feldman and Yair Wallach, '"Zionist Pawns", Old Prejudices and Pop Star Cabals: Inside the UK's Big Antisemitism Blind Spot', *Haaretz* 9 December 2021, in which the JDA is invoked in an apparent justification of Miller's termination.

56. In '"Zionist Pawns"', written after Miller's termination, Feldman and Wallach criticize the way in which the JDA was used to argue against termination. The authors seem to imply that an accurate application of the JDA would have resulted in Miller's termination. Feldman makes clear in his public writings that he considers Miller

and his supporters to be engaged in uncritically promoting anti-semitic tropes. What is less clear is what kind of action Feldman thinks should be taken in response to that. In David Feldman, 'The David Miller Case: A Textbook Example of Anti-Zionism Becoming Vicious Antisemitism', *Haaretz*, 4 March 2021, he acknowledges Miller's right to academic freedom without actually defending that freedom.

57. This argument is developed in detail by free speech theorist Eric Heinze in articles such as 'Viewpoint Absolutism and Hate Speech', *Modern Law Review* 69: 4 (2006).

58. Author's conversation with David Miller, 4 December 2021.

59. As has been established, this dictum – which first appeared in S. G. Tallentyre, *Helvétius: The Contradiction. The Friends of Voltaire* (London: Smith, Elder, & Co., 1906), p. 199 – actually originated with Voltaire's biographer Evelyn Beatrice Hall, who wrote under the pseudonym S. G. Tallentyre.

60. 'Investigation Carried Out under the University of Bristol's Ordinance by [redacted] QC', paragraph 31. This document was leaked by *The Electronic Intifada* ('Second Bristol Report Exonerated David Miller of Anti-Semitism', 26 November 2021) following the disclosure of parts of the first report (authored by the same QC).

61. 'Investigation Carried Out under the University of Bristol's Ordinance', paragraph 31, at tinyurl.com/3nd636wa. Emphasis in the original.

62. In 'The David Miller Case', Feldman refers to a 2013 paper co-authored by Miller 'which speculated that Zionist donors had suborned Labour's foreign policy under Tony Blair's leadership'. Feldman states that there was 'no evidence to support this suggestion, he conceded, but this didn't inhibit his conjecture.' Hence, Feldman acknowledges the long history of Miller's views, and implicitly accepts that the problem is not limited to Miller.

63. This is the approach suggested in Rebecca Ruth Gould, 'The Limits of Liberal Inclusivity: How Defining Islamophobia Normalises Anti-Muslim Racism', *Journal of Law and Religion* 35: 2 (August 2020).

Epilogue: Who Is a Jew? Personal Reflections on Jewish Questions

1. 'A Call to German Parties Not to Equate BDS with Anti-Semitism', joint letter, *Haaretz*, 3 June 2019 – at haaretz.com.

2. David Feldman, 'The Real Reason Corbyn's "Anti-racist" Labour Just Can't Deal With Anti-Semitism', *Haaretz*, 27 November 2019.

3. Author's correspondence with Maciej Wzorek, Coordinator for the Genealogical Database Dissemination Department, Muzeum Historii Żydów Polskich POLIN, 5 January 2022.
4. Some of Stern's writings in this vein include 'I Drafted the Definition of Antisemitism. Rightwing Jews Are Weaponizing It', *Guardian* 12 December 2019; 'Written Testimony of Kenneth S. Stern, Hearing on Examining Anti-Semitism on College Campuses', 7 November 2017, docs.house.gov/meetings/JU/JU00/20171107/106610/HHRG-115-JU00-Wstate-SternK-20171107.pdf; and 'Will Campus Criticism of Israel Violate Federal Law?', *New York Times*, 12 December 2016. For a critical review of his book *The Conflict over the Conflict*, see Tom Sperlinger, 'Is There a Crisis of Antisemitism in Higher Education?', *Times Literary Supplement* 6, 129 (18 September 2020).
5. Important scholarly works that are notably silent on this issue include Keith E. Whittington, *Speak Freely: Why Universities Must Defend Free Speech* (Princeton: Princeton University Press, 2018); Nadine Strossen, *HATE: Why We Should Resist It with Free Speech, Not Censorship* (Oxford: Oxford University Press, 2018); and Eric Heinze, *Hate Speech and Democratic Citizenship* (Oxford: Oxford University Press, 2016).

About the Author

Rebecca Ruth Gould is the author of numerous works at the intersection of aesthetics and politics, including *Writers and Rebels* (2016) and *The Persian Prison Poem* (2021). With Malaka Shwaikh, she is the author of *Prison Hunger Strikes in Palestine* (2023). She has written for the general public in the *London Review of Books*, *Globe and Mail*, and *World Policy Journal*, and her writing has been translated into eleven languages.